Time in Indian Cultures
Diverse Perspectives

Time in Indian Cultures

Diverse Perspectives

Editors

Priyadarshi Patnaik
Suhita Chopra Chatterjee
Damodar Suar

D.K. Printworld (P) Ltd.
New Delhi

Cataloging in Publication Data — DK

[Courtesy: D.K. Agencies (P) Ltd. <docinfo@dkagencies.com>]

Time in Indian culture : diverse perspectives / editors, Priyadarshi Patnaik, Suhita Chopra Chatterjee, Damodar Suar.

p. cm.

Contributed articles.

Includes bibliographical references.

Includes index.

ISBN 13: 9788124605356

ISBN 10: 8124605351

1. Time management — India — History. 2. Time — Religious aspects — Hinduism. 3. India — Civilization. 4. Philosophy, Indic. 5. Time in literature. 6. Time in art. 7. Vedic literature — History and criticism I. Patnaik, Priyadarshi, 1969- II. Chopra, Suhita, 1959- III. Suar, Damodar, 1954-

DDC 294.5440954 22

First published in India, 2009

ISBN 13: 978-81-246-0535-6 (HB) ISBN 10: 81-246-0535-1

Published and printed by:
D.K. Printworld (P) Ltd.
Regd. office : *'Srikunj,'* F-52, Bali Nagar
Ramesh Nagar Metro Station
New Delhi – 110 015
Phones : (011) 2545 3975; 2546 6019; *Fax* : (011) 2546 5926
E-mail: dkprintworld@vsnl.net
Web: www.dkprintworld.com

Contents

Introduction

I

TIME pervades the Indian psyche: its presence is both experienced and debated in this tradition. *Kāla*[1] is a word which is familiar to most Indians and is used variously to mean time personified, time as death, time as the supreme reality, time as a cycle, time as the appropriate moment, time as destiny and so forth. A number of other words like *samaya*, *ṛtu*, *velā*, *ākāśa*, *kṣaṇa*, *muhūrtta*, *ghaḍī*, etc. are also used either to refer to time or to its different aspects.

While *kāla* is the generic expression for time, it occurs only once in the *Ṛgveda*, and that too in a later section. To the early Vedic agriculturalists and herdsmen, time (*ṛtu*) meant a settled point of time, time appointed for any action (especially sacrifices or worship) and a division of year (seasons).[2] In the *Atharvaveda* and the Brāhmaṇas *ṛtu* was gradually superseded by *kāla* — a word derived from *kal*, meaning to calculate or enumerate. Time is mentioned in the *Śvetāśvatara Upaniṣad* (Section 1.2) in the context of explaining the nature of *Brahman* and some passages in the *Maitrī* (Section 6.14-6) refer to it as well. *Atharvaveda* also refers to *kāla* in the context of its ability to "create" the world:

---

1. *Kāla* and many compound words using *kāla* are very common in many Indian languages — *kālacakra*, *akāla*, *nityakāla*, *dīrghakāla*, *sarbakāle*, *kalekāle*, etc.

2. Monier Monier-Williams, *Sanskrit-English Dictionary*, Delhi: Motilal Banarsidass, 1899, rpt. 1993.

> . . . the *Atharvaveda* has two hymns (19.53, 54) where, among other things, it is said that time created both heaven and the various firm grounds that lie beneath (*AV* 19.53.5ab: *kāḷo mūṁ divam ajanayat kāla imāḥ pṛthivīr uta*) and that it gave rise to creatures and Prajāpati (19.53.10ab: *kālaḥ prajā asṛjata kālo agre prajāpatim*).[3]

While a number of words are used to connote the general concept of time such as *ṛtu*, *muhūrtta*, *veḷā* and even *ākāśa*, *kāla* is most frequently and widely used and we shall often use it to refer to time. For instance, *kāla* generally refers to a "fixed point of time," or "right time," "a space of time," and "time (in general)" in *Atharvaveda* and *Śatapatha Brāhmaṇa*; "the proper time," "the time for departure," etc. in *Śatapatha Brāhmaṇa* and the *Mahābhārata*. Again in the *Mahābhārata* it is used in the sense of "occasion," and "circumstance." It is also used in the sense of "a period of time," "time of the world" (or *yuga*), "measure of time" (in prosody), "death," "time of death," etc. in various other texts.[4] Such a wide range of meanings of time point to two things: (1) the difficulty in grasping and defining time (which is debated and discussed in Indian thought), and (2) the different fields in which *kāla*, as a concept (or as different concepts), plays a significant role, namely, the Purāṇas, Grammar, Philosophy, Astronomy, Jyotiṣa (astrology), Dharmaśāstras and Nītiśāstras (precepts), Vāstu (architecture), Saṅgīta (music), Citra (painting), Sthāpatya (sculpture), Āyurveda (medicine), etc.

Time forms an inevitable part of discussion of any ancient tradition. This is true of India where one sees discussions of

---

3. George Cardona, "A Path Still Taken: Some Early Indian Arguments concerning Time", *Journal of the American Oriental Society*, vol. 111, no. 3 (July–September, 1991), pp. 445-64. fn. p. 446.

4. Monier Monier-Williams, op. cit.

two aspects of time — time in the phenomenal world (*saṁsāra*), and Time unaffected or beyond this world (timeless) as in *mokṣa*. Both this-worldly activities and time, and time's transcendence (*mokṣa* or *nirvāṇa*) are found in almost all philosophical as well as religious traditions of India.[5] Ananda Coomaraswamy refers to this division of time into "time" and "timeless" in the Vedas, the Upaniṣads and Āraṇyakas as well as the *Mahābhārata*. He writes:

> In *AV*.19.53 and 54 [*Atharvaveda*], cited above, "Time" — absolutely — is the source of all relative times; not itself a duration, but rather the Timeless, Eternity, to which all moveable time is ever present. It is in these terms that the *Maitrī Upaniṣad* distinguishes the "two forms" (*dve rūpe*) of *Brahman*, i.e. aspects of the two natures (*dvaitibhāva*) of the single essence (*tad ekam*), as "time and the Timeless" (*kālas-ca-kālas-ca*).[6]

This attitude gets further reflected in almost all aspects of Indian tradition and culture. For instance, in Indian aesthetics, when Abhinavagupta talks of the concept of (*ātma*) *ānanda* or *camatkāra*, a transcendence of time is suggested. Aesthetic relish or enjoyment is like no ordinary enjoyment. It is like *brahmasvāda* (the experience or relish of *Brahman*) — a state of bliss that "doesn't depend upon past or future time."[7] This presupposes two levels of transcendence of time — (1) of real "temporal" time as one moves into the world and time of the

5. Brian Smith, "Time" *New Dictionary of the History of Ideas*, ed. Maryanne Cline Horowitz et al. (Thomson Gale, 2005), p. 2332.
6. Anand Coomaraswamy, *Time and Eternity*, Switzerland: Ascona, 1947, p. 15.
7. From *Locana* quoted in Kulkarni's *Outline of Abhinavagupta's Aesthetics*, Ahmedabad: Saswati Pustak Bhandar, 1998, p. 55.

work of art, and (2) a move from the world and time of the work of art into a "timeless" state wherein *rasa* or aesthetic enjoyment takes place in a transcendent present or "now." Such an approach affects the diverse art forms.[8]

An interesting trend about India's approach to time has been observed by Brian Smith. According to him:

> As opposed to modern notions of the progressive nature of time, traditionally in Indian texts time is envisioned as degenerative and entropic. Such a viewpoint on the nature of cosmic time goes all the way back to the early Vedic cosmogonies where the universe is said to have been created by a god (Puruṣa, the Cosmic Man, or Prajāpati, the "Lord of Creatures"). The work of creation, however, was defective. The creator "emits" from himself the creation, but in this cosmogonic move from primordial unity to multiplicity and diversity the product is characterized by disconnection, confusion, and disarray. The very parts of time are, in their original state, created in a "disjointed" manner: "When Prajāpati had emitted the creatures, his joints became disjointed. Now Prajāpati is the year, and his joints are the two junctures of day and night, of the waxing and waning lunar half-months, and of the beginnings of the seasons. He was unable to rise with his joints disjointed.
>
> — *Śatapatha Brāhmaṇa* 1.6.3.35[9]

Another remarkable aspect of Indian notion of time is its cyclic nature. Transmigration of the soul suggests a cycle of birth and death, but not in replicative temporality (i.e. one doesn't go on endlessly living the "same" life again and again in

8. Although critics might point out that Abhinavagupta was primarily talking about plays and that poetics should not be confused with aesthetics, one cannot deny the fact that Abhinava's poetics significantly affected thought about the various art forms like dance, music, sculpture and painting.
9. Brian Smith p. 2332.

different births). But even this "apparently forward moving time" in which cycles of births and deaths take place itself is subject to some kind of transmigration — "Just as souls were perpetually reborn, so was the universe and time itself."[10] Interestingly, this cycle is degenerative and cyclic at the same time.[11] But since it is eternal, it is regenerative as well and hence *sṛṣti* and *pralaya* follow one another endlessly. Interestingly, the disjointed time of the Vedas and the Āraṇyakas which constantly needs repair (provided by rituals) or which would lead to entropy[12] later gets reflected in the entropic tendency of the *yugas* (aeons) which move from purity to impurity (at least in the way they are presented, for instance

---

10. Brian Smith p. 2332.

11. The first of these is the "Golden Age" or *Kṛtayuga*, which lasts for about 4,000 divine years (each divine year is the equivalent of 360 human years), a period of happiness and great virtue. The next two aeons, the *Tretā* and *Dvāpara*, are both shorter (3,000 and 2,000 divine years, respectively) and increasingly worse as all things, including lifespans and the human's capacity for spirituality, decrease. The process culminates in the last and "dark" or *Kali yuga*, which is identified always in these texts as the present age of utter degeneration. At the end of this final aeon (which lasts 1,000 divine years), the world will end in a cataclysmic apocalypse. After a period of dormancy, the universe will be recreated and the process will begin again . . . endlessly." Brian Smith p. 2332.

12. "With the *Agnihotra* [the twice-daily sacrifice performed at dawn and dusk] they healed that joint [which is] the two junctures of night and day, and joined it together. With the new and full moon sacrifices, they healed that joint [which is] between the waxing and waning lunar half-months, and joined it together. And with the *Cāturmāsya* [performed quarterly at the beginning of the seasons] they healed that joint [which is] the beginning of the seasons, and joined it together. (*Śatapatha Brahmana* 1.6.3.36)" Brian Smith, p. 2332.

in the concept of the *yugas*, where one moves from the *Kṛta* aeon of purity to *Kālī/Kali* or the dark aeon of dissolution) in the Purāṇas and in Sāṁkhya literature as well.

Māyā (referring to the illusory or ephemeral nature of the world) is another important concept that pervades much of Indian thought and has implications with reference to how we look at time. While saying nothing new it emphasizes the strong contrast between "time" (where things happen, which is the medium in which *māyā* enacts itself) and "timeless" which is beyond all notions of past, present and future and hence established in *mokṣa* or *nirvāṇa*.

However, one must be careful of the cyclic time *vs*. linear time, and East *vs*. West kind of oversimplification. In fact, the West looks at this over-generalized Hindu notion of cyclic time as theoretically weaker — since "linear time better reflects lived experience."[13] However, as discussed earlier, the cycles of birth and death are not identical or self-similar, and hence allows for linearity. This point needs clarification — while transmigration implies the cycle of birth and death, what happens in each birth is different, and hence, if we assume continuity, in that continuity, time and events move forward in linearity.[14] Thus, the Hindu notion of time allows for both for cycles of lived experience (in each birth) as well as continuity (of *karma*), and linear time as well.

Though time figures somewhere or the other in most of our ancient texts starting from the Vedas, and in spite of the

13. Anthony Good, "Congealing Divinity: Time, Worship and Kinship in South Indian Hinduism", *The Journal of the Royal Anthropological Institute*, vol. 6, no. 2 (June, 2000), pp. 273-92, 280.

14. Good uses the metaphor of a rotating wheel (which completes cycles and moves forward at the same time) as opposed to a spinning disk (which suggests self-similar cycles of rotation). p. 281.

fact that time plays such an important role in Indian culture and society, it is interesting to note the paucity of significant philosophical treatises that focus on time or *kāla per se*. The six schools of philosophy — Vedānta, Sāṁkhya, Yoga, Mimāṁsā, Nyāya, and Vaiśeṣika — do not discuss it in much detail. It figures in Vaiśeṣika and Nyāya. The concept of dependant origination, *pratītyasamutpāda*, in Buddhism, talks of 12 stages which include past, present and the future, and the momentariness (*svalakṣaṇa*) of everything also problematize time,[15] and the Mādhyamika school takes it up for a more detailed discussion. The Cārvāka are concerned with the hedonistic present. The Jainas also discuss time rather marginally. However, it is only with the fifth century CE philosopher of language, Bhartr̥hari that we have the first extant text a section of which is entirely devoted to *kāla* — *Kālasamuddeśa*. Yet, on the whole, time doesn't get that kind of attention in Indian philosophy as it gets in many Western traditions.

But, it would be wrong to say that there is absolutely no discussion on time in Indian thought. As George Cardona points out, we have arguments ranging from the "very general to the particular" about time in Indian philosophy. It is discussed in grammar, in Nyāya and Vaiśeṣika and also in Buddhism. While Vaiśeṣika and Nyāya accept time as a distinct substance (*dravya*):

> It serves as the cause for certain caused knowledges: relative proximity or removedness independent of spatial relation, simultaneity, non-simultaneity, long duration and quickness of actions. Such knowledges require a cause that determines them, so that, by virtue of implying such a cause, they are "marks" (*liṅgāni*) which make known time as an

15. This will be discussed in some of the essays that follow.

> entity to be accepted. In addition, it is accepted that — as opposed to direct perception, which has as its possible object only a presently existent something — inference applies to objects connected with any of three time divisions, past, present, and future, so that it can make known what is not now existent by virtue of being past or yet to come. Accordingly, three time divisions are accepted.[16]

There is a lot of debate in both grammatical and philosophical traditions about present time (*vartamāna kāla*), while past and future pose no problem — since "becoming" and the ephemeral present are difficult to grasp both in language and in the phenomenal world. As a consequence, continuity *vs.* discreteness of time is also an issue that is debated in our ancient tradition.

So why is it that *kāla* finds no sustained place in Indian thought, while it pervades our culture and tradition? One of the possible reasons could be because of its cyclic as well as infinitesimal nature. The other could be because of the firm belief of most schools of thought in the transmigration of soul and rebirth. Linear time, in many non-Hindu traditions, even if infinite, is irrevocable. It is a road where one cannot turn back once more. Such a time presents a crisis of eternal loss, of never being able to go back. However, in cyclic time one always comes back (a new start or rather, a new kind of continuity),[17] there is one more time; if something is incomplete this time, it can be done the next time — time doesn't pose a

16. George Cardona, "A Path Still Taken: Some Early Indian Arguments concerning Time", *Journal of the American Oriental Society*, vol. 111, no. 3 (July–September, 1991), pp. 445-64.

17. It is like a game which can start all over again. You can learn from your mistakes and improve your game. The idea is to reach a point where you don't have to play any more — *nirvāṇa*. Although you can play the game once more, the games are not self-similar.

crisis of loss, nor does time "run out." It is possible that this could be one of the reasons for the lack of much exploration of time in Indian thought — probably because much of it is taken for granted and it is not considered "problematic."[18] The other reason could be the nature of focus of most schools of Indian thought. While Buddhist and Jaina traditions were primarily ethical in nature, the six schools of Indian thought explored the nature of ultimate reality. The ephemeral is suspect, or else it does not matter. The anxiety of time does not exist. If traversing to the other realm is not possible in this birth, there is always a next birth. Hence time is not an issue, and "Time" is equated with *Brahman*. This is not to say that philosophical explorations were not there; it is only to point out that they were not as detailed or exhaustive as in many other philosophical traditions.

Much of what is discussed in the context of Indian thought gets reflected in different socio-cultural practices. But many newer dimensions of time are also explored and referred to in such contexts. The Vedas show an obsession with longevity — One prays for progeny and for a long and healthy life. This is later reflected in Āyurveda which prescribes the means for a healthy and long existence. Even today, when elders bless the young (even on such common occasions as formal greetings), they often say: "May you live to be a hundred years."

Another important notion that pervades Indian culture is the notion of the "irresistibility" of time. In the opening chapter of Ādi Parvan of the *Mahābhārata*, the bard Sañjaya consoles the grieving Dhṛtrāṣṭra with the declaration that all creatures

---

18. Although *vartamāna kāla* or present time and its existence is rigorously debated in grammar, Nyāya, Vaiśeṣika and Buddhsim.

pass from birth to death and then to rebirth through the irresistible operation of Time. It is *kāla* that ripens the creatures and then rots them.[19] Śaṅkarācārya, in his *Mohamudgara* refers to the way time steals everything away in moments (*nimeṣe harītam kāla sarvam*). It may be noted that the Western agony is at the poignancy of a short life at the end of which there is only death and oblivion. The Indian agony is not so much because of the shortness of life as for the endless repetition of life, death and suffering (*kālacakra*) from which freedom is so difficult to achieve. Coming back to the issue of irresistibility, if Time is irresistible, then events in Time also share the same characteristics. It is thus, that, in Indian culture *kāla* is also equated in many contexts with destiny and fate (*daiva*).

A third interesting notion related to time in Indian socio-cultural context is the notion of "appropriateness of time." Since the microcosm is an integral part of the macrocosm, it becomes logically necessary that human actions be placed in the context of the cosmos — the stellar bodies, the various landmarks, objects, shadows (solar and lunar eclipses or Rāhu and Ketu), etc. Time is not a mere abstract shell in which things happen. It takes into account the very spatial configurations of which it is the cause. The temporal moment has a spatial counterpart in terms of planetary positions and also *nakṣatra*s (asterisms) and hence plays a significant role in determining the aptness of the moment. The significance of this kind of time (*muhūrtta*) can be understood from the fact that we have, at a later date, innumerable Muhūrtta-śāstras or treatises that deal with appropriate time. In fact, all the Śrautasūtras, including Dharmasūtras (books of law or morals) and

19. There is in fact a specific word that highlights this aspect of time — *kāladharma*. It implies the rule, law or operation of time, as well as the influence of time on material objects. See Monier Monier-Williams, op. cit.

Gṛhyasūtras (rules of domestic life) are also greatly dependant on the Muhūrtta-śāstras in the context of starting or ending any particular action. In the *Rāmāyaṇa* the notion of *muhūrtta* is explicated with interesting examples. The *Rāmāyaṇa* refers to particular *velā* in the episode of the Jaṭāyu. When Rāma meets the dying bird, Jaṭāyu reassures Rāma that Sītā would be restored to him since she was stolen at a *muhūrtta* or time when, if a thing is lost, it is recovered.[20] At places, in our cultural lore, to reap the maximum consequences of one's action one must act at the appropriate moment. Thus, in the *Rāmāyaṇa*, we find Rāma making a *liṅga* out of sand and completing the installation ceremony. He was forced to do so since the appropriate *muhūrtta* was passing and Hanumān was late in fetching a *Śivaliṅga*.[21] In everyday life too, the idea is highly valued and action must be regulated in terms of appropriateness of time. Notion of birth and death must be regulated by the appropriateness of time. Sexual union must also be at the appropriate time and season (*ṛtujuṣ*), so that birth can be at the right time. Every activity of one is marked by appropriateness. The notion of appropriateness pervades virtually all walks of life including medicine (the appropriate time for plucking plants, preparing and administering medicine, etc.) and arts.

In the Indian science of space or architecture (Vāstu),[22] the notion of Time comes in for an elaborate discussion, not only in the context of appropriateness but also in positing the relation of Time (*kāla*) with space (*vāstu*). In fact, the science of

20. *The Ramāyaṇa*, Aranya Kāṇḍa, 67th canto.

21. Gayatri Devi Vasudev, ed., *Vāstu, Astrology and Architecture*. (Delhi: Motilal Banarsidass, 1998) p. 172.

22. *Vāstu* is derived from the word *vas* meaning to dwell. Branching out of sculpture, the science of Vāstu or Śilpaśāstra finds numerous references, implicit and explicit, in the Vedas, Brāhmaṇas, Upaniṣads and Purāṇas.

space can be understood only with reference to the science of Time (*kāla*). *Kāla* is the element emanating from the primordial energy. This energy exhibits in terms of vibrations and time vibrations cause the emanation of form. This can be explained with the help of music. Just as the vibrations of a string instrument cause the emergence of sound spaces, imposition of discipline on the frequency of vibrations leads to a variety of sound forms. Further order imposed on vibration leads to rhythm or *tāla*. The rhythm-bound sound spaces turn into sweet musical forms. The same unit of time or rhythm can be extended to the evolution of material spaces into spatial forms, such as temples, building, etc. These are all examples of rhythm-bound material forms.[23]

Thus, while in philosophy time as past, present, future; as duration; as transcendent was important, in socio-cultural and ethical life, what played a more important role was the concept of the appropriateness of time — *muhūrtta*. Out of it the notions of purity and impurity in relation to time — *śubhamuhūrtta* (auspicious time) and *aśubhamuhūrtta* (inauspicious *muhūrtta*) also emerged.

While this brief discussion attempts to touch upon some of the important concepts of time in our tradition, there is much that is either not presented here, or is still to be explored, be it in our tradition or our contemporary socio-cultural milieu. It is this realization that has provided impetus for the present volume. The essays collected here attempt either to re-analyze and bring into focus and interpret earlier explorations of time, or else they attempt to give form to and bring into awareness usages and practices in various walks of our thought and tradition that have direct bearing on the notion of time/Time.

---

23. Vasudev, op. cit., p. 35.

II

The papers in this volume belong broadly to two categories. The first section presents papers which broadly deal with the philosophical, religious/spiritual or linguistic aspects of Time. The second group of papers deals with time in Indian culture and society, art and music, and contemporary culture.

Professor P.K. Mukhopadhyay's seminal paper, "Does Time have a Beginning? — Some Inter-systemic and General Reflections," starts by examining time in apparently diverse fields, namely cosmology and philosophy. He begins by pointing out that time has been discussed variously in diverse fields and yet any discussion of time is replete with confusions, ambiguities and misunderstandings. Since time is conceived of and articulated differently in different disciplines, is a dialogue among them possible? Professor Mukhopadhyay feels that it is not only possible, but also necessary in order to dispel much of scientism and soft spiritualism which exist in science and philosophy in relation to time. The paper first addresses the issue of the compatibility between modern cosmological view of time with its emphasis on the origin of the universe at big bang, and Christian theology which also suggests that the universe has a definite beginning and that God creates it. In spite of the apparent compatibility, are they really confirming each other's world views? This is the first question which is taken up. After exploring some of the inconsistencies that emerge out of this debate, Professor Mukhopadhyay attempts to test an Indian theory of time — from Nyāya viewpoint — in terms of its validity and internal consistency. In the process he also raises certain fundamental questions about how time is defined and how it is measured in various traditions including Nyāya. If not challenge science, he at least indicates that there are alternative ways of formulating world-views other than using science — i.e. by using philosophy and linguistics. Although it is not spelt out, what underlies such an analysis is the assumption that the very conceptualization of the world, even by a cosmologist, is via language. Similarly, the methodology of analysis, logical rigour and examination of validity and consistency are strikingly similar both in cosmology and philosophy. It is on the basis of this that the paper is able to compare the notion of the beginning of time in the contexts of cosmology, theology and philosophy. The paper concludes by raising certain fundamental questions about the notion of progress and development. In the framework of linear time — a gift of modern science — human progress is a linear unending process. In an ever expanding universe time is without an end. We move on endlessly towards refinement along the graph of progress. And yet, this notion of progress and human refinement, which is based on the notion of time according to cosmology, is an uneasy fit since this goes against the grain of the arrow of thermodynamics which talks of increasing atrophy with time. He compares this world-view with the Nyāya world-view (in a certain sense, representative of Indian world-view) where progress is non-linear and cyclic. A detailed, stimulating and thought-provoking paper, it sets the tone for the various papers to follow which examine time from diverse other perspectives.

Professor S.K. Saha's lucid paper, "Time and its Knowledge" which follows, first puts his discussion of certain philosophical aspects of time in context before presenting certain arguments about time from Nyāya-Vaiśeṣika perspective — especially in the light of the arguments of Gautama and Vātsyāyana. Professor Saha begins by quickly giving an overview of different Indian perspectives on time. He points out that according to the Buddhists, time is momentary — nothing more than discreet moments. According to the Jainas time has slices, can be added endlessly, and yet is not infinite since it is made of composites and "nothing composite can be infinite as its limits are, theoretically speaking, identifiable." Professor Saha, thus, suggests that in spite of effort on the part of certain other Indian philosophers to suggest that time is one and infinite, there are many alternative views as well. He then attempts to point out how the Vaiśeṣika view attempts to resolve the point by saying that time is infinite and yet it has slices. The notion of slices brings in the issue of past, present and future, an issue debated again and again in many philosophical traditions around the world. The "present" is problematic according to the Buddhists, and Professor Saha attempts to present Gautama and Vātsyāyana's attempts to resolve the crisis and argues that present time exists. Most philosophers who subscribe to the presence of past and future use a spatial analogy — a falling body. At any point of time, past is the line that has already been traversed by the object, and future the time yet to be traversed. Hence, there is no need for the present. Gautama points out that the spatial analogy is not apt for examining time; and time and its uniqueness can only be caught by focusing on "activity." Next paper focuses on Indian arguments pertaining to perception and how through these theories the perception of time can be established. Vātsyāyana uses grammar (we believe under the implicit assumption of an organic relation of the word and the world) "that the verbs used in the other tenses in similar types of statements refer to actions which have already been completed or are still to be completed, thus indicating the existence of the past and the future, which refers to past, present and future." Besides, all knowledge and perception take place in the "present." Next, Professor Saha asks, how one perceives time? Answering it by saying that it is done directly the way we know ourselves, he points out that the ancients have also extended a similar logic: *pratyakṣa pramāṇa* (direct perception) may take place without the use of the senses, as is the case when we are aware of ourselves, and this is known as *saksi jñāna.* The same is also true of time.

Next we move on to language and time. Time comes to us essentially through language. Professor Patnaik looks at the use of the concept of *kāla* by Bhartṛhari (a philosopher of language) from a broad perspective in her paper, "Time as Power: A Brief Survey of Bhartṛhari's Metaphysics." Focusing on why the six schools of philosophy do not make use of time as a pivotal concept, she points to the sequential nature of communication and the unfolding of meaning in time as the chief reasons for Bhartṛhari's use of it in *Kālasamuddeśa.* Professor Patnaik tries to locate the metaphysical implications of Bhartṛhari's conception of *kālaśakti* that serves as a link between the two opposite metaphysical constructs, i.e. *śabdatattva Brahman* and the phenomenal world; the former eternal and non-sequential and the latter changing and sequential. Bhartṛhari introduces the concept of time as power (*kālaśakti*) to bridge the conceptual gap between the two as he presents the phenomenal world not as the concatenation of substances (as the Vaiśeṣika believes) but of events and processes (*jagat prakriyā*) that is characterized by sequence (*krama*) and not as a series (as the Buddhists conceive). His conception of time is closely connected with his philosophy of language that delineates one and the eternal language-principle (*śabdatattva*) as manifesting itself in the form of sequential human speech. So, time is seen as the basic conceptual apparatus that serves as the link between his view of metaphysics as well as semantics.

We articulate and conceptualize it in words and words contain within them the temporal implications of time. Dr Ganesh Prasad Panda, in his short paper entitled "A Perspective on Time in Language and Grammar," focuses on the way nouns, verbs and roots play a significant role in the denotation of time in sentences. Taking the sentence as the basic unit of communication, he illustrates his point with eleven types of sentences and the way the sense of time (past, present and future) is communicated through them. Each sentence stands for a category or mode through which time is communicated in Sanskrit.

Language has philosophical, commonplace and poetic uses. Professor Niranjan Mohanty's[24] paper, "Time in Indian Spiritual Traditions and its Representation in Indian Poetry: A Study," tries to show how philosophical issues are made manifest in the creative process. Professor Mohanty approaches the Indian notion of time in terms of the Western notion of binaries. He attempts to point out the binaries are discernible in the Indian context as well — namely, Time/time. Eternal time or the timeless is contrasted against the notion of time which pervades our lives, in which everything takes place. According to Professor Mohanty, this "autonomous construction of binaries" generates debates and often leads to confusion rather than clarifying issues. And yet, the two are intrinsically linked. For instance, it is only through "time" that one can understand or realize "Time." In the second part of his paper, he talks of Indian poets from different periods (Sālabega from the sixteenth century, and Tagore and Ramanujan in the twentieth century) whose poetical works show the contrast and tension that exists among these two concepts of times in such concepts as physical/spiritual, mortal/immortal and time/timeless — a tension that is generated and ultimately resolved by the artist who intuitively experiences this crisis, presents it and

24. It is sad Professor Mohanty is no longer with us. He passed away in 2008.

attempts a harmonization or resolution of it in his/her work of art.

In the second section of the book time is discussed in the context of the world of material, social and cultural existence. This gets reflected in the papers that are collected under this section. Dr. Brinda Paranjape begins her paper, "Time in Indian Traditions: A Note on the Mahābhārata," by asserting that even today, clock-time has hardly any relevance for the majority of (illiterate) Indian mass. However, time is experienced, in relation to the seasons, time to sow seeds, new moons and full moons, and its impact on one's social, cultural and physical life. The other, conceptual notions of time that seep into the minds of common people are through the Itihāsa-Purāṇas like the *Ramāyaṇa*, the *Mahābhārata* and the numerous Purāṇas. Taking up the *Mahābhārata*, Dr. Paranjape illustrates different attitudes or concepts of time that can be constructed by interpreting the biographies of some of its central characters. For instance, Vyāsa who is immortal represents man's wish for eternal life, while Bhīṣma shows "the limitation of sensory perception which is related to human form." This is so, since Bhīṣma is a cursed *vāsu*, born to Gaṅgā, who can only be released by death from the bondage of life and death. On the other hand, Kṛṣṇa *avatāra* (who spells the beginning and end of one *yuga*) or incarnation includes both death (because he is born and dies) and deathlessness (because he is God). In the final count, according to her, "Time" is experienced, and through the *Gītā*, a "theistic understanding of the Time" becomes "the base of the spiritual life in India, distinctly far from the mechanized reckoning of time of the modern world."

Dr H.S. Komalesha and Dr Jaison A. Manjaly, in their paper "Concept of Time in India: A Literary and Philosophical Understanding," critique the Western notion of history (which is one way of capturing past time) as well as Western notions that India never really knew how to document history (which presented her as culturally inferior). They ask, "what is the necessity of invoking chronology/time if at all our sole aim is to evoke the past to influence our present and shape the future?" In the post-colonial context the attitude of the West to the Indian sense of history or lack of history reeks of imperialism. Dr. Komalesha and Dr. Manjaly point out that in India history is internalized in "a creative fusion of fact and fiction, myth and reality" in "those societies where myths and legends are the cardinal methods of recording the experiences of the past." This indicates differences in approach — while for the West it is important to document past in a scholarly and "objective" way, for India it is important to transmit and hand down to later generations the moral lessons learnt from that past. While history reminds us of the past, creative works make it almost a lived experience. Briefly referring to the Indian philosophical tradition they point out that "memory," so relevant for history, is not considered a source of valid knowledge in Indian philosophy, and hence undermined. Such a stand has its own richness and needs to be appreciated.

Next we move on to music. Professor Sushil Kumar Saxena, in his short paper "Time in North Indian Music," while focusing on the role of *tāla* (rhythm) and *laya* (aesthetic pace), also tries to explore the relation of time (time sense) in the real world to time in the world of music. Saxena begins by justifying discussing time in relation to music: "What exactly is the warrant for relating rhythm with time? My ready answer is: the fact that the two share some features visibly. Time flows, so does music." He refers to the cyclic nature of beats which correspond to clock-time in a certain sense. Talking about the beats themselves, he discusses the intricacies of north Indian rhythms and points to how time makes itself felt or is experienced in terms of rhythm. Often, certain parts of the rhythm are virtual since they are not played (but called out in the *bola*) and yet their presence is accentuated by their marked absence during the actual performance. At other points of time, the way one reaches the *sama* (or the beat where the cycle and the patterns all attain to completion of their individual forms) draws attention to the aesthetic beauty of that micro-second or time instant — another interesting way of experiencing time through music. Relating musical time to lived experience, Professor Saxena points out that "successiveness, or the before-after order, is not the only feature of lived time that the art of rhythm builds upon." But referring to debates about real time and musical time in Western aesthetics, he points out that in spite of these similarities, experience of real time and musical time need to be differentiated the way it is experienced in Indian music:

> Would it make sense to deny the distinctness of sweet from salted food on the ground that they are both known by tasting? It is . . . not how we experience them, but what exactly we experience in them that make the two orders of time quite different from each other.

This is followed by a creative exploration of time by Dr Bimal Mohapatra whose "multimedia" presentation of time in this book is unique because it presents an artist's way of looking at his work and its relation to time. His text and visuals, "Time: Representation in Form," is important since it represents the reflective process about time and its relation to art in retrospect — by looking back at his own work and at the artistic process in general after it has been competed. Focusing on the relation between time and creation, in a few words, and by using his own illustrations and paintings, Dr. Mohapatra explores the creative, generative process and the way it associates itself with time — the movement from chaos to flux.

The paper that follows also discusses painting, but from a historical perspective. Dr Priyadarshi Patnaik's paper, "Time and the Rāgamāla Painting Tradition: A Brief Exploration," emerges from within both a cultural and philosophical exploration of the notion of time in the Indian context. It shows how time makes itself felt in the Rāgamālā paintings through their intrinsic relation with music. *Rāga*s are meant to be sung at specific times of the day or night; similarly each season has its own *rāga*s which are appropriate to it or evoke its moods. Rāgamālā paintings, which emerged, interestingly, in the period of Muslim interaction with Hindu culture (of *khayāl* tradition in singing and court miniature paintings), often take as their inspiration *dhyāna śloka*s (a tradition which is around a thousand years older) which are Sanskrit (and later Hindi) verses that describe the *rāga* (male) or *rāgiṇī* (female) as a personified image. Often, the iconography of these images is faithfully depicted in the paintings and the sense of the appropriate time or seasons depicted or suggested through sky, trees, flowers, birds and other such natural details. Dr. Patnaik suggests that the notion of cyclic time, of suggestion (through appropriate representation of skies, birds or flowers), of appropriateness of time, all get embodied in this artistic tradition which flourished from the sixteenth to the nineteenth century CE.

The visual and deeply experiential form of architecture is presented in the next paper. Dr Joy Sen and Dr Joydip Dutta's "Time and Architecture — Dialogues" focuses on the way time is perceived in Indian architecture. They suggest that Indian architecture has the ability of making one experience time in a very profound way. According to them, "architectural space may be considered to have four successive hierarchical experiential stages in this continuum of space-time." Indian architecture is essentially symbolic and aims to make manifest the ideational behind the material. In architectural space-time, one moves from the outer to the inner sanctum, from the material to the spiritual, from time to timelessness. This journey is made manifest in various ways through Indian architecture. They illustrate this with the help of philosophical concepts that are internalized in Indian architecture.

The final paper by Ms. Dr. Amrita Basu, like Dr. Mohapatra's, deals with contemporary culture. While Dr. Mohapatra explores his personal experience as an artist with time, Ms. Basu focuses on time in popular culture, especially popular song tradition which also includes visuals. This admits film songs and music videos, both of which are telecast in dedicated music channels and in other entertainment channels as well. Ms. Basu's paper is insightful in trying to point to the way the notion of time is absorbed into popular music through a process of enculturation. Certain popular cultural notions related to time — the notion of rebirth and the notion of appropriateness — also find place in Indian popular music. As illustrated by her, they often figure in the narratives of the songs through lyrics and visuals. The notion of time ingrained in Indian music through *rāga*s meant for appropriate seasons and times of the day also find a place in popular songs where, if seasons or specific diurnal times are to be evoked, songs are set to the apt *rāga*s. Ms. Basu also looks at the way cinematic devices — colour *vs*. monochrome visual images — are used to refer to time in many such songs. But her paper also shows an awareness of decontextualization of time that often takes place in popular culture. Time out of context and a disregard for time also forms a part of this treatment, as is pointed out by her.

We hope that this small but rather unique collection of papers would stimulate our readers and make them explore the notion of time in various other contexts in our philosophy, culture and society.

June 2009

1

Does Time Have a Beginning?
Some Inter-systemic and General Reflections[1]

P.K. Mukhopadhyay

I

Cultural Perspective and Theoretical Studies

WE argue that for theoreticians of any particular discipline — be it science, philosophy or theology — it is both a general cultural obligation and useful practice to be alive to the state of knowledge, including past achievements and new advances in the neighbouring theoretical areas. Sometimes from such a source one may derive the needed insights or clues and at other times motivation or reasons for formulating, reinterpreting, or modifying, as the case may be, one's own theory. Alternatively, one may oneself suggest to one's counterparts in other disciplines some new challenges and critiques that may lead to the further development of those areas. In this connection we should remember the important remark recently made by the celebrated physicist Wheeler.[2] He said, ". . . Philosophy is too important to be left to the

1. It is supposed to be the revised version of what was once presented in a Seminar on Time organized at IIT Kharagpur. But after too radical a revision it has now become altogether a new paper.

2. In his article "How Come The Quantum: Can Philosophy Help?", *Science Philosophy Interface*, (1996) vol. I, no.1, John Archibald →

philosophers." It is certainly true but it holds equally good, with suitable adjustments, for any specialized study including science, though science has comparatively far shorter a history. However, what Wheeler said is of special importance for us as it refers to the context of modern cosmology.

Interdisciplinary exchanges are rare and there may be many reasons for that, but hardly ever did the great experts of theoretical disciplines doubt or deny their usefulness. Sometimes what prevents the thinkers of one field to take cognizance of what is happening in other adjacent areas is the pressure of attitudes like scientism and mysticism. Most of the theoreticians in the forefront of their disciplines, including disciplines like scientific cosmology, which will figure more in our discussion, are found to be free from such pressure. But even then many among those who accept in principle the usefulness of knowledge of adjacent areas and of conversation beyond the barrier of individual disciplines, cannot often translate what they believe into action because of the systemic obligation of specialists to pursue their study in isolation and at a high degree of technical sophistication unintelligible to

---

→ Wheeler, the celebrated physicist, writes, "since 1988 I have been bewitched with two questions of still more difficult cast: 'How come the quantum?' and 'How come existence?'." He thought that a really talented researcher could "ask me to discuss some of the wonderful foundation stones of cosmology and quantum theory as we see them today." "It would be an even grater challenge and joy to ferret out to discuss every clue and every writer in every domain of thought that promises significant insight on "How come existence?" and "How come the quantum?". Wild goose chase? Find out which are wild geese and which is the Merlin with a revelation to disclose! And argue that philosophy is too important to be left to the philosophers. Search out potential clues in the fragments that come down to us from the writings of the pre-Socratic philosophers and some of the later thinkers."

even specialists of other fields, let alone interested public.[3] This is as truer about mathematical physics as of Navya-Nyāya or even analytical philosophy or some recent theological writings. But there are always some, actually very few, in almost each specialized field, who love to take extra burden on them and speak and write beyond the narrow boundary of their respective fields of study. They do a great service both to the subject they represent and the culture and the people, to which they belong, as a whole.

Our present treatment of the subject of time will quite naturally reflect some of the remarks made above. It will not be too technical or mathematical[4] and within the limited area to be covered in our discussion on time, which is otherwise a very vast subject, we would conduct a non-specialist study of some of the wider implications of a highly developed and incredibly technical discipline, the modern scientific cosmology. In this we will follow the lead of some great experts of this field who did display their awareness of the implications of their research on human progress and Christian theology in particular. We will also consider the implications of modern scientific cosmological thinking on philosophy and social thinking and will study the relevant issues from the perspectives of both Christian and non-Christian cultures. Even

3. Cf. Stephen W. Hawking, *A Brief History of Time: From the big-bang to the Black Holes* (Bantham Books, 1988), p. 185.

4. Those who think only mathematical treatment of a subject is analytic and exposition that uses formulae are only precise are correct to some extent only and need to be reminded of that Ludwig Eduard Boltzmann (some of whose works are directly related to some of the themes of modern cosmology we will discuss here) is reported to have said that the true theoretician makes only sparing use of formulae. It is only in the books of the allegedly practical thinkers that one finds formulae only too frequently, and used for mere adornment.

so we have not endeavoured to achieve the impossible and cover all the issues. For example we have completely omitted the important and interesting area of discussion, namely, consciousness or experience of time. The discussion of the few issues selected here is not thoroughly comprehensive or correct in every technical detail. Our purpose has been to share with the readers how these issues are related or at least how they can be related to us. Had it not been so we would not have felt so intrigued, worried or interested in the issues or spent time discussing them. It intrigued us, for example, how the big-bang cosmology could be claimed to be in line with the Christian theological account of the origin of the universe or of time. Similarly we find it to be a great problem how the cosmological interpretation of the arrows of time and the scientific defence of them can be reconciled with the modern ideology of progress. If these are our critiques of modern cosmology we also endeavour to examine here if and how far the Indian system of thought known as classical Nyāya can accommodate some of the basic findings of modern cosmology in its otherwise theological cosmology.

Our discussion is not meant to be either historical or literary. Rather it will be philosophical and analytical. It will also be philosophical in the broader sense of theoretical enterprise called on to provide rational foundation — explanation and justification — of the beliefs and practices of a people. So cultural perspective matters for theoretical studies since at one end it necessitates such studies and at another end it suffers from the implications of the findings or conclusions of these studies. Theories of time are among the best examples to illustrate our point. Time, a very vast, intricate and rich subject, is a matter of specialized and technical investigations of varying degrees of sophistication as well as a matter of wide and general concern. At one end it permeates the whole of our ordinary life, experience[5] and language and at the other end it forms the subject matter of one of the most advanced and technical areas of contemporary physics. It not only fascinates romantic poets but also seriously engages unrelenting intellectualists. It is a matter of equal concern for rationalists and mystics. It seems that the discussion of time can even be a case study in (A) (i) (intellectual) cultural divergences, (ii) conversation among cultures (such as ancient Greek, medieval Christian Europe, modern secular and scientific Europe, and the *vaidika* India) as well as sub-cultures within these cultures (such as science, religion and philosophy).

Incidentally, the discussion on time again can prove to be (B) a needed corrective of many popular and not so popular mistakes and misunderstandings that have led to and fed such stances as scientism on one extreme and soft spiritualism verging on a debased or shallow form of mysticism on the other. For example, it is a popular scientistic belief that religion has no place in the age of science; that science is the whole of human knowledge,[6] that everything in science is analytic, empirical and rational whereas in metaphysics everything is

---

5. Anindita Niyogi Balslev has quoted in her book, *A Study of Time in Indian Philosophy* (Wiesbaden: Otto Harrassowitz, 1983), p. 9, the following passage from an unidentified source: *na so 'sti pratyaya loke yatra kālo na bahasate.*

6. Hilary Putnam, *Mathematics, Matter and Method* (Philosophical Papers, vol. 1, 2nd edn.), (Cambridge University Press, 1975), pp. xiii-xiv. "It will be obvious that I take science seriously and that I regard science as an important part of man's knowledge of reality; but there is a tradition with which I would not wish to be identified, which would say that scientific knowledge is all of man's knowledge." "If the importance of science does not lie in its constituting the *whole* of human knowledge, even less does it lie, in my view, in its technological applications." See also Wolfgang Smith, *Cosmos & Transcendence: Breaking Through the Barrier of Scientistic Belief* (Sherwood Sugden & Company, 1984/ 1990), pp. 9-10.

speculative and in religion it is mythical or mystical; that the history of philosophy is the history of endless battles and disagreements among philosophers which lead us nowhere whereas science[7] gives us definitive knowledge and generally accepted truths. The fact, however, is different. In theology and more so in any developed philosophy there are a number of definite and settled doctrines each of which has enjoyed down the centuries support, though not unanimous, of a large number of thinkers. Also we very often find quite rigorous and good, from even the scientific point of view, arguments, even if not necessarily scientific arguments, in philosophy and even theology. We cannot simply dismiss, without serious consideration, philosophical or theological critique of cosmology, which is not an impossibility or rarity. On the other hand, within a short history of about four hundred years modern science has radically changed its views about time, and in cosmology the scientists are still debating as to which is the best model of the universe, the steady state, oscillating or the uniformly expanding? The reply that the last is the choice of the largest number of scientists can hardly score much. For first, we can cite the example of string theory, which seems to be welcomed and opposed by equal number of great scientists today.[8] Secondly, persons who are in a position to know say that there has been significant decline in recent time in the culture of rationality even as science has grown at a very fast pace.[9] Lastly, it has also been said that scientists are

7. Note the singular.
8. Cf. P.C.W. Davies and J. Brown, (eds.), *Superstrings: A Theory of Everything* (Cambridge University Press, 1988).
9. See P.K. Mukhopadhyay, "Realism and Some parallel Problems of Epistemology and Methodology of Science" in M. Bandyopadhyay (ed.), *Nyāyavasiṣṭha* (Kolkata: Sanskrit Pustak Bhandar, 2006), pp. 526-41, for the relevant quotations from Popper and Hanson Norwood Russell.

not above human frailties and that support to many theories at times depend on extra theoretical considerations.[10] The compensatory stance of the soft spiritualists and shallow mystics who dread or deride the very idea of intellectual enterprise — such enterprise is a veritable hindrance to man's higher quests; modern science in particular, is thoroughly materialistic and narrow, cannot accommodate or do justice to other aspects of life and proved in recent times to be too demonic a power which if unchecked will lead to total destruction of the entire human race — is equally mistaken and, in our opinion, more pernicious for society at large. Besides, there are attempts to make us believe that India's characteristic attitude to science is no other than what is just described and that her perspective is essentially spiritual and mystical. Facts as well reason tend to show that this is not true. The fact is that in India soteriological practices and the quest for "mystical" experience developed simultaneously and in mutual harmony with the vigorous intellectual enterprises and explorations, in diverse fields, that carried out investigations that are empirically constrained and rationally consistent. Only soft spiritualism and the culture of excessive cultivation of emotions on the one hand and shallow and debased mysticism on the other are averse to an analytical theoretical pursuit. The representative Indian doctrine of mysticism, if we are allowed to use such an expression, does

---

10. J.V. Narlikar said. "Scientists do not know the answers to puzzles like these which may call for radical rethinking. Indeed, howsoever objective they may call themselves, the practitioners of science tend to be reluctant to face new evidence that forces them to revise their ideas. Thus many of the puzzles are simply wished away." Quoted in Arpita Chattopadhyaya and P.K. Mukhopadhyay, "The Creation of Matter: Traditional Thinking and Modern Science", in *Science Philosophy Interface* (Calcutta, 1996), vol. 1, no. 2, p. 45.

indeed lay great importance on transcending time and the temporal — in the sense of the ephemeral and transient — but it does not prescribe the path of mysticism for all or at the initial stage. For the majority of people and even for the qualified few, at the initial stage of their development, other pursuits are both helpful and often necessary.

The right type of intellectual pursuit for some time helps rather than hinders the mystic aspirants in their quest for the transcendental goal.

Here are the related questions and implications that one would like to discuss in connection with time today. We will elaborate on only some of them. We would like to begin with a question, which may appear thoroughly technical and exclusively scientific. But, as we shall show, this also has rich cultural implications and that precisely adds to the interest the question has for us. The scientific question is about the beginning of time — (i.a) does time have a beginning? We will see that this question has, through the related question about the origin of the universe — [(i.b) does the universe have a beginning?] — wide-ranging implications. Discussion about the origin of the universe is found not only in mythology and theology but also in philosophy and science. But in these sources the origin or otherwise of time is not as frequently or separately discussed. The answer to these two related questions which scientific cosmology, based on recent scientific findings, offers has been noted to have profound implications for theologies and philosophical cosmologies of different times and cultures. It is the obligation of the concerned individuals to answer the questions, "If and how can one reconcile with or accommodate in one's cultural vision, world-view or philosophy either the recent scientific findings in question or the scientific theory based on them?" and "Whether one's needs must modify or abandon one's own theory?" However, taking a third perspective we can suggest what would seem to us to be the possible right course to take for some of the different systems of thought. The point we want to emphasize is that the answer from the concrete cultural background — whether it is a particular or narrow theoretical discipline or more wide socio-philosophical vision within which that discipline developed — has great importance; sometimes these answers may appear to be preferable to abstract and technical ones. Scientists, Christian theologians and papal authority have actually considered and answered these two questions. But their answers to the question as well as the question itself need further critical examinations from within their system of thought and also from the points of view of other relevant cultures and theories — non-Christian theology, philosophy and culture. In this connection we would discuss the question, (ii) Can Christianity accommodate recent scientific findings or, to put it differently, is Christian theology scientifically confirmed today? The same question could be asked with reference to other theologies also. The same question, whether time has a beginning, can be discussed in theistic theologies and related philosophies, without necessarily involving reference to science, and secondly in philosophy as categorical or conceptual study, without necessarily involving reference to either science or theology. So far as the first context is concerned there are theologies like the Christian theology and maybe some philosophy as well, which admit both that time is created and that God has created it. In the majority of Hindu theologies and certainly in Nyāya philosophy time is held to have no beginning though simultaneously creator God is admitted there. Who holds such a view is immaterial. The question is, can a theory that does not admit that time has a beginning be rationally justified? It goes against both modern cosmology and Christian theology. But is that a sufficient reason to dismiss it? One thing is certain, to dismiss the theory for that reason is not half so theoretically rewarding as to search for what compelling reasons led one to propose or uphold such a theory. If the subject of time does not allow us to raise and discuss these issues then, theoretically speaking, it is of little interest. It may turn out that any technical discussion such as the one from the point of view of modern cosmology can hardly be communicable and interesting beyond the narrow limits of astrophysics. Anyway, the question is (iii) "Is it possible to admit both that time is eternal and that God is a creator?" The dominant science or scientific cosmology contends that time is created but it neither asserts nor denies that God has created it. This has actually been strongly interpreted, sometimes at least, by both the concerned scientists and Christian theologians to suggest that the present scientific theory of time is compatible with Christianity or the (theistic) theological cosmology of the Christians. But on closer examination it will appear that there is really no compatibility here. The scientific theory of creation in question conflicts with the Christian doctrine of God. And the Christian theological as well as the scientific cosmological views that time has a beginning conflict with such theories as admit that time is eternal. Some may think, and it is serious, that the wider implication of modern scientific cosmology is that both theological cosmology of the Christians and philosophy or philosophical theology of, say, Nyāya are under severe threat of being disproved on strong scientific ground.

There is however a danger here. The confidence some people seem to express, that it is theology or philosophy — and not science — which is under the threat of falsification due to the incompatibility in question, seems to have an element of scientism or science-worship in it. We have already discussed above the issue involved here. It should be noted further that sometimes the questions of compatibility, incompatibility, rational choice, vindication or falsification, as the case may be, are discussed in the abstract and limited context of a certain system or theory only. But we need to consider the issue in the larger socio-cultural contexts as well. We just cannot dismiss it as irrelevant or weak if it is shown that a certain scientific theory or truth conflicts with some foundational belief or presupposition of the very culture within which it emerged or that it is not in harmony with other sub-cultures, within the same super culture, which authentically reflects and is compatible with the overall cultural vision of the people in question. For example, if a sub-culture turns out to be not only in conflict with other sub-cultures but also in disharmony with the culture within which it is a sub-culture or if it falsifies the very foundation on which the entire social structure — social perceptions, policies and institutions of that culture — is based, then we have to think twice before we decide to accept that dissenting view just because it has a label: scientific. It is not suggested that there may not ever be the need or necessity to radically revolutionize a certain culture but what is suggested is that the acceptability of a scientific theory should not be based on the pseudo-scientific attitude called scientism or even merely on the strength of *theoretical* virtues such as internal consistency, experimental confirmation, simplicity and the like. We also need to examine carefully larger socio-cultural implications. If it is not to be pursued as merely an intellectual game or exercise in technical expertise then the theoreticians of any field — philosophy, science or even theology — should remain alive to the question of the origin in and wider impact on respective cultures of their theory. In particular we cannot afford to follow blindly certain scientistic pronouncements and beliefs like "the only good explanations are those that we find in established sciences." We will have occasion below to explain this point a little more and ask ourselves the question (vi) Can we find in areas other than science, say in rational theology or philosophy or religion, explanations that are as good as those that we find in established sciences? Are there theories or views that enjoy such explanations even though they otherwise conflict with scientific theory?

We would like to end our enumeration or identification of issues with a philosophical question that is philosophical in the broader sense of philosophy stated earlier. The question relates to the connection between certain conception of time and the ideology of progress. We ask among other things, "Is the current cosmological sense or interpretation of time consistent with the ideology of progress which almost defines the modern scientific culture which in a sense has allowed this cosmology to emerge?"

One objection: It is already clear that there are different views or theories of time and they can have wide ranging implications. So it is desirable that there should be some comprehensive and realistic study of time that will pay attention to the socio-cultural contexts in which the related questions arise and to the broader concerns of people on which any answer would have its impact. Normally, discussion in any single discipline of knowledge or department of culture cannot but have some implications for the related investigations and theories of other such disciplines or departments.[11] This does not mean that we just cannot hope to make a start in our discussion on time, first because we are to comprehend such a wide scope, and second, there are

11. Thus entropy, which was originally a concept of thermodynamics, was later generalized and given physical interpretation and incorporated in mechanics. The process of generalization did not stop there. It is now an important notion in Information theory.

unmanageably many divergences and a great many concerns. We have already given one answer to this sort of objection. Some aspects of these different conceptions of time or alternatively some features of time under all the different conceptions are the same.[12] It is not our intention to say that we cannot study the problems and theories of time of any particular discipline without studying the related problems and theories of all the other disciplines. It rather means that our study of a certain phenomenon should begin by studying the relevant question, which is a characteristic question of that particular discipline. Then we should relate what we thus learn to the problems and theories about the same or related phenomenon that are characteristic features of some other discipline. For example, it is not a characteristic question or problem of the discipline called contemporary scientific cosmology whether time has a beginning or not. For the theoreticians of this field there is no doubt that time has a beginning.[13] But the really characteristic problem of this new scientific cosmology is how to relate meaningfully and defend the conception of time that emerges within the big-bang theory to theories of entropy increase and problems of choosing one from three different models of the universe: the steady state, oscillating, and uniformly expanding. For the sort of comprehensive study we have in mind, it is also desirable to inquire about the impact or implication this cosmology has with regard to the characteristic question of history and culture study. For history and culture study, one important question

12. For example that time has its own definite direction is admitted by all even by the scientists even though it is difficult for a scientist as scientist to distinguish past from future or vice versa.

13. And for another reason also it is not an issue in science in general; for, in science time means measurable time and the non-eternity of such time is never seriously doubted.

is, "How different conceptions of time shape and are shaped by different ideologies of progress?" And this question may be, through such other question as whether time is linear or cyclical, related to the pertinent question of technical importance whether the universe has a boundary or not. Similarly one characteristic question of philosophy as a conceptual study is what is the logic of "creation" or of "time" and other related words or temporal predicates? On the other hand, whether God makes Himself a prisoner of time by creating it is more characteristically a question of theology.

II

Cosmology and Theology

It is intriguing to note that while cosmogony was one of the first disciplines of knowledge to develop in human history; scientific cosmology did not really begin before 1970 or before vigorous search for GUT began. Among Ionian thinkers, in the mythologies of different countries, epics and scriptural literature, we find thinking and discussion on the origin of the universe and its constituents. Not always are discussions in such literature clear and definite. The issues are often not precisely or clearly formulated. Even today some questions lack adequate clarity. For example, what could possibly be meant by the phrase "origin of the universe"? Is it one single thing, which we can see or hold in its entirety at any moment such as say, a clay doll? We can ask about the origin of so many particular things like the Suez Canal or systems like stars and galaxies or species like human beings or subjects like cosmology, all within the universe, but it makes little or no sense to ask about the origin of the universe itself and as a whole. When it comes to the universe as a whole it is better to hold that it is always there, though within it things are occurring, changing and getting destroyed. Suppose we have answer to the question about the origin of all the identifiable things and processes of the universe, does then there remain anything more to be asked? So in the context of the question of origin we can hardly mean by the word universe anything other than the totality of each and every created thing or effect within the universe.[14] One may also wonder why a person should ask in addition the question about the origin of the universe itself.

Besides the problem about the meaning of the question, one may also ask about the possible motive or reason behind the inquiry into the origin of the universe as a whole. Is there any good reason or motive to ask about the origin of the universe? It is also sometimes seriously doubted if scientists can justify their cosmological inquiry or more particularly their search for what is known as the Grand Unified Theory. Hawking[15] has tried to answer this question in his own way and with reference to GUT. Another completely different and characteristically Indian way of answering the question may be found in a philosophical text of the Nyāya system of thought. The work under question is better described as philosophical theology as it deals with the rational proofs for the existence of God. It has been said in this text that to ask the question of the origin is to ask about the cause. The motive behind asking about the origin or the cause of the universe (*jagat*) is that if of the two alternatives of having and not having a cause we opt for the second then that would imply either that the universe is fictitious or it is always there.[16] If there is any special reason why we should want to avoid each of these

14. In Sanskrit (*Saṁskṛta*) language the word for the universe often has this sense. It is almost uniformly the case with the philosophical writings in this language.

15. Cf. Hawking (1988), pp. 13-14.

16. See Udayanacarya, *Nyāya Kusumañjaliḥ*, prose text introducing the verse 1/4.

alternatives, then that would count as a good reason for holding that the universe has a beginning. To put it differently, it makes good sense to ask the question about the origin of the universe since we cannot admit either that the universe is as unreal as square circle or that it is eternal and is always there. But if we cannot ask and answer the legitimate questions about the beginning of the universe — such as when did it begin, how did it begin and the like — then its impermanence would remain just a presupposition or unargued assumption. And now that there is a good reason to ask about the origin of the universe it becomes all the more necessary to be clear about what the question "Does the universe has a beginning?" can really mean. For, even then the origin of the universe could not necessarily mean the origin of the universe as distinct from all things within the universe. Further we can hardly ask about the origin of everything in the universe. It is possible to hold that unlike many other things of the universe space and time are just there; they are not created. "Furthermore the space through which atoms move, and the time by which their progress is gauged, lay outside the scope of the theory entirely. Space and time were regarded as simply there, not themselves part of physics. In these respects, then the work of Galileo, Newton and Laplace could not be considered to constitute a very satisfactory TOE."[17] Generally speaking modern science usually avoided the question of origin as such which, perhaps for that very reason, is commonly held to be a question for speculative metaphysics, if not poetry, to ask. The other reason is that before the prediction of Doppler Effect, development of general relativity, (not the special theory of relativity), and Hubble's observations there were no good scientific reasons why scientists should bother about the origin of the universe

17. P.C.W. Davies, and J. Brown, *Superstrings: A Theory of Everything* (Cambridge University Press, 1988), p. 3.

or of space or time. Since it became a genuine scientific question and the search for an answer was found also to hold the key to finding GUT some physicists proposed the big-bang theory. According to this theory time no longer means an absolute or eternal time. The only time these physicists know of is the time that was created along with the universe at the big-bang. So only after 1920s (as a matter of fact long after that year) science found acceptable reasons to raise the question about the origin of the universe. Till then the question about the origin was the concern of the speculative philosophers or metaphysicians on the one hand and of theologians on the other.[18] This is in short the answer to the question why scientific cosmology emerged so late.

But then we have the other question, what does "origin of the universe" mean? We understand that only recently the scientists have observational evidence that the universe is not static but is changing or is being created. So only now they can ask when its creation started and how? But have we made any advance in understanding what the creation of the universe means? The answer is decidedly yes. It now has very definite sense which is at the same time somewhat different from the sense given to it in some earlier philosophical works. It means creation of the elementary particles, atoms, the physical forces, the laws of physics, time and space and stars and galaxies, almost in this order.[19]

For the universe is created at the big-bang singularity and before the big-bang there was nothing. No elementary particle,

---

18. "When most people believed in an essentially static and unchanging universe, the question of whether or not it had a beginning was really one of metaphysics or theology." Hawking, 1988, p. 8.

19. Hawking 1988, p. 124f. also see Boslough, *Stephen Hawking's Universe* (Avon Books, 1985), p. 75 and p. 80f.

no space, no time,[20] no physical forces or laws, no prediction and of course no observer or observation.[21] This is in a sense creation out of nothing as it has even been said in so many words in works like *The Second Creation.*

> On the far side of the big-bang is a mystery so profound that physicists lack the words even to think about it. Those willing to go out on a limb guess that whatever might have been before the big-bang was, like a vacuum, unstable. Just as there is a tiny chance that virtual particles will pop into existence in the midst of subatomic space, so there may have been a tiny chance that the nothingness would suddenly be convulsed by the presence of a something.[22]

Does it appear like talking in metaphors? Well that is almost always the case when we talk about time. And it is theoretically inescapable when we are talking about the far side of the big-bang.

Anyway, to the question, when did the universe begin the, answer is at the big-bang. But what is this big-bang? A very precise answer is possible and has actually been given. It is "singularity at the beginning of the universe." And what is singularity? That too can be described without metaphor and with mathematical precision — incidentally, it is, as Hawking said, a mathematical concept[23] — it is a point at which the

---

20. We will see that this is a non-standard use of the word creation. In some other context creation means bringing together pre-existing stuff of the universe such as *paramāṇus* to form the first created material thing. And this creation is creation in time and by some one.

21. See R.P. Crease, and A.C. Mann, *The Second Creation* (Chapter 19) (Indian edn.) (Delhi: Affiliated East-West Press Pvt. Ltd. 1987) and Hawking (1988), chapter 8.

22. Crease and Mann (1997), p. 405, emphasis added.

density of matter and space-time curvature became or was infinite.[24]

To return to our main question, when did time begin? The answer is, at the big-bang. For non-specialists it may prove a bit difficult to make sense of the statement "Time began at the big-bang time." It will be at least psychologically more satisfactory if we formulate the position in this way "There was no time before the big-bang." It avoids the rather tricky and embarrassing question, is big-bang itself a (point in) time?

It should be possible to express both the thesis about the origin of time and the grounds supporting it in a way that even the non-specialists can understand them to the extent necessary for conversation across the boundary of the otherwise extremely specialized discipline of modern scientific cosmology. There are a number of very good as well as bad works, as Hawking has noted, which answer to this need.

Anyway, science or the scientific theory in question cannot really tell us, let alone prove, that before the big-bang time or the universe was not there. All that it can say is that we cannot make any sense of the expression "before the big-bang. . . ." Nor does it find any need to admit that there was a universe or time before the big-bang. Scientists have no *use* for such supposed state or truth. One may say that all that this shows is that a scientifically satisfactory explanation of the evolution of the (material) universe does not have to refer to a state *before* the big-bang.[25] Even so, one would like to continue. Neither any scientist nor anyone who is not seized by scientism

23. Hawking (1988).

24. It is perhaps the lack of scientific boldness or philosopher's fastidiousness that makes us hesitant to describe singularity as "A point in space-time at which the space-time curvature is infinite."

25. Strictly speaking that would be also meaningless.

has any reason to say such a state was not or could not be. Lack of utility of something, and that too in a certain particular context, is no logical ground for admitting the non-existence of it. However, it is not very difficult to decipher the real point of the scientist. He would say that the question of the existence of a thing that cannot be even described or expressed intelligibly does not arise. The putative time before the big-bang is just such a thing.

However, "time" and related expressions like "past," "present" and "future" all have clear sense in scientific language.[26] In science we may say past refers to the time marked by the occurrence of an event or state of a thing that is retrodictable. Similarly the future is that time which is marked by the occurrence of an event or certain state of thing that is predictable.[27] Thus in science "time," "past," "present" "predictability" are all related. None of these expressions can have a clear and acceptable sense in science if that renders the other related expressions meaningless. When we qualify time by the putative property "before the Big Bang" we cannot make sense of, say "predictability," etc. This is why scientists should think that we have no cogent reason to accept time that existed, if it really existed, before the big-bang. But we can make perfect sense of "time" and the other related expressions if we take time after the big-bang. So far it will

26. We will see that contrary to what many think, this is also largely true about commonsense and ordinary language. The scientific sense of time stated here will be found to tally closely, up to certain point at least, with the sense the word has in its commonsense use.

27. One may find, if one carefully considers it, that this attempt to determine the future and the past in terms of predictable event and retrodictable event is grossly defective. But we will not go into that.

not be rational or scientific to hold that time existed before the big-bang. This seems to be the intended paraphrase of what the big-bang cosmologists mean when they say that time has a beginning and it began at the big-bang. Stephen Hawking beautifully makes this point.

> This means that even if there were events before the big-bang, one could not use them to determine what would happen afterward, because predictability would break down at the big-bang. Correspondingly, if, as, is the case, we know only what has happened since the big-bang, we could not determine what happened beforehand. As far as we are concerned, events before the big-bang can have no consequences, so they should not form part of a scientific model of the universe. We should therefore cut them out of the model and say that time had a beginning at the big-bang.[28]

> At the time called the big-bang the universe was infinitesimally small and infinitely dense. Under such conditions all the laws of science, and therefore all ability to predict the future, would break down. If there were events earlier than this time then they could not affect what happens at the present time. Their existence can be ignored because it would have no observational consequences. One may say that time had a beginning at the big-bang, in the sense that earlier times simply would not be defined. . . . It would be meaningless to suppose that it (the universe) was created before the big-bang.[29]

So far it seems that the model of the universe according to which the universe is expanding and the big-bang theory, which contends that the universe and time had their beginning at the big-bang, best explain the observations, made by

---

28. Hawking (1988), p. 50.
29. Ibid., pp. 9-10.

Hubble. And within the limit of observational consequences and empirical predictability, science can make no sense of a time that is supposed to have existed before the big-bang. This is so far the meaning of saying that time is created at the big-bang.

We started with the observation that we could not say that time had a beginning and was created at the big-bang simply because science had no use of a beginningless time or it could not make any sense of the expression "time before the big-bang." And after going through the accounts of the scientists we came to conclude that unless we could find some other sense of time, which is equally definite and intelligible, then the only rational thing to do is to accept that time had a beginning; and it began at the point it did because we could not make any scientific sense or use of any time before this point. We would presently discuss some other senses of time. However, let us for a while discuss about some of the possible and actual responses to this scientific theory of time. To be more concrete, what, if any, has been so far the response to this theory or the discipline of cosmology of which it is a part, from such other sub-cultures as theology, philosophy and the like. Nobody should suspect that we are attempting to force the cosmologists into a discussion with the theologians. This is not so. For as a matter of fact many scientists and general public as well as the Catholic Church are already found to be acting in this direction in some sense or other. Some are very hopeful and go as far as to proclaim that modern cosmology confirms Christian theology. Some are of the firm opinion that "the world-view endorsed by the physical sciences since the time of Galileo is incompatible with the Christianity's traditional world-view."[30] An author of this view hoped that

30. This has been the opinion of W.T. Stace. Similar points have been made elsewhere also. In his *Cosmos and Transcendence: Breaking* →

the European public and the Christians would readily endorse and generally accept his point. However, the violent response he received proved shocking to him.[31] This shows that the majority thinks either that the cosmological view could be assimilated or accommodated into Christianity, which in any case is scientifically confirmed by the findings of modern cosmology, or that at least some dialogue would be possible. In fact Christianity has changed much of its earlier positions in view of, or as a result of accommodating, new discoveries of the developing sciences.[32] Hardly anybody today believes that the whole of the Bible should be taken literally, that it should be accepted that the universe or the world was created only about 5000 BCE. It may seem that science can also accommodate God and religion. At least it is no part of the activity of good science to deny God.

If we now ask a cosmologist what would be his term for a dialogue and reconciliation, he would be likely to say that creation of the universe or time by God, as Christianity preaches, would not conflict with modern cosmology if God creates the universe obeying the physical necessity identified by cosmology, that is, if God creates the universe at the big-bang.[33] But this would amount to putting a restriction on God's omnipotence and unlimited freedom to act — the features,

---

→ *Through the Barrier of Scientistic Belief,* its author Wolfgang Smith writes, "So far as cosmology — Weltanschauung in the literal sense — was concerned, European civilization became de-Christianized." p. 142.

31. See J.W. Smith, "Stace, Walter Terence", in Paul Edwards (ed.), *Encyclopedia of Philosophy* (Macmillan Publishing Company, 1967/ rpt. 1972), vol. 8, p. 3.

32. One may profitably read in this connection J.J.C. Smart's paper "Religion and Science" in *Encyclopedia of Philosophy,* vol. 7, pp. 158-63.

33. Cf. Hawking (1988), p. 10.

which are undeniable in the Christian religion. So just by noting the similarities that like modern cosmology Christianity also admits that the world has a beginning and on the basis of the fact that cosmology does not say explicitly that God has not created the universe, one should not jump to the hopeful conclusion that the two are compatible. We do not know exactly the content of the 1951 official pronouncement in which, Hawking says, the Catholic Church declared that the big-bang is in accordance with the Bible. On the other hand, there are those who dislike the big-bang model because, by admitting that the universe and time have a beginning, it makes room for divine intervention in creation seem to us a bit alarmist. To us it seems that the theses of absolute creation and of a God who is eternal and the omnipotent creator are inseparable parts of Christianity and these have really no place in the cosmology we are discussing. It does not follow from this alone that anyone of these two theories is false or weak. However, if we take these discrepancies seriously we may be led to inquire if any revision or reinterpretation can, while strengthening the theory or theories in question, show that here there are just explainable and intelligible differences but no real conflict. For whereas no theory at any point of time is beyond improvement so also within the unity of the culture and cultural perspective in which they emerged there is likely to be differences without incompatibility. We should not however, play down genuine conflict as mere difference nor should we magnify a genuine difference and present it as a conflict. We intend to use this occasion as an opportunity to examine both the hope expressed in favour of Christian theology and if this theology is self-consistent. We have already said why modern cosmology does not seem to be compatible with Christianity. Now we turn to examining if it is self-consistent.

III

The Paradox of Creating Time

Once we accept that the cosmological theory is consistent we, thereby, commit ourselves to considering any theory to be weak, to say the least, if it conflicts with the cosmological theory. We have seen earlier that this is exactly the case with the Christian theory. Now, in continuation of that, we want to test the Christian theory for its self-consistency. This theory contends that time has a beginning and also that God has created it along with the universe. However, His creating time is found to be incompatible with God's omniscience, omnipotence, immutability and eternity. We will not discuss whether it follows from the conception of absolute creation, as the divine creation is admitted to be, that time is also created by God. But it is admitted that God is the creator of time also.[34] Now it is a part of the general conception of God (or of creator God) that he is omnipotent. Besides, in the majority of the systems of thought and in all of the systems that we study here, God is also the creator of the universe. If one does not believe in God one does not need to admit a creator God either. It also seems to be quite consistent to think that a creator God must be omnipotent (as well as omniscient) as otherwise we could not credit Him with creating such a vast, complicated and well organized universe as the one in a part of which we live. But do we need to admit that this omnipotent God is also eternal? It seems that the answer must be in the affirmative. For, otherwise we would need another creator to create the universe along with its non-eternal creator — a position that is untenable for many reasons. We will not pursue this matter here, instead we will admit, as is done usually, and we have not heard of any non-eternal God, that God is

34. See, for example, P. Edwards (ed.), *Encyclopedia of Philosophy*, vol. 2, p. 255.

eternal too. There are, however, two other features of this created universe that seem to conflict with God's omnipotence. We will not discuss here the first one — the presence of evil in it — that is being widely discussed since long past in connection with the problem of evil. The other feature is time itself, which seems to permeate the whole universe. We do not know of any theory of creation in which time does not figure. In the Christian theology moreover this time is itself created by God. Nobody has seen Him create time, but the argument[35] is that if he did not create it then it would not be a feature of the created universe or God would not be omnipotent. This much is fairly clear, at least to a Christian. But the Christian God should have seen in his infinite wisdom the problem that He was creating by creating time. At least man in his finite wisdom finds here a problem. God's creating time conflicts with His eternity, omnipotence and omniscience — all of these. For once He creates time He is no longer the Lord of it but becomes subject to or is affected by temporality; He loses His immutability and hence eternity. But why does He lose omniscience and omnipotence?

It will be found that God cannot be eternal and affected by time at the same time. If He is eternal, as He obviously is, He remains so even after He creates the universe. His very eternity makes him immune to change or mutability. This argument takes for granted that eternal means timelessly eternal or outside time. Any completely transcendental God would be eternal in this sense. But there are two questions: first, "Is there any other sense of the word eternal?" and "Is timelessly eternal in the accepted Christian sense of the word eternal when it is applied to God?" It is known that some neo-Platonists find that the timelessly eternal sense is more acceptable, for the other sense conflicts with God's

---

35. As it stands it need not be a sound argument.

immutability. However there are others who think the sense of eternity, which comes closer to the Biblical use of the term, is everlasting (in time). Further, there is no unanimity that Christian God is completely transcendental. Be that as it may, we take here the second sense of eternity to be the standard Christian sense on the authority of scholars like Swinburne.[36] It comes to this then that God who is eternal and the creator of the universe is everlasting in time, the time He creates. This means He is in all periods of time past, present and future. However, God cannot be related to past, present and future, in any familiar sense of the term, without losing His omnipotence and omniscience. On the other hand if God suffers the loss of these properties due to His relation to time then He suffers change and is no longer immutable or eternal. Let us, following Swinburne, elaborate the point a little.[37]

Periods of time — past, present and future — can be distinguished if there are different events in relation to which or by descriptions in terms of which they can be picked out. Time that can be picked out by the only identifying description "time before creation"[38] is not made up of or divisible into different periods of time. Within the created universe, however, we can pick out different periods of time in terms of different distinguishable events.[39] Before creation we could

36. See Mohapatra et al. (eds.), *God, Time and Evil, The Swinburne Lectures*, Utkal (University) Studies in Philosophy (Bhubaneswar: Utkal University, 1992).

37. See P.K. Mukhopadhyay, "Rationality and Religion" in Mohapatra et al., (eds.) (1992), pp. 68-83.

38. Provided, of course, there is or even could be, according to the Christian theology, such time.

39. It is not clear whether this amounts to saying that by relating one single pre-existing time to different distinguishable events we introduce different periods of time. But this is very important. Anyway Nyāya is very clear on this point.

not have different distinguishable periods of time, as there would be no events and hence no distinguishable events either.

> Periods of time are the periods that are in virtue of the actual or possible events which end or begin when they begin, or end or begin when they end; and instants are the points of time which are the boundaries of such events. By a 'possible event' I mean some event of a specified kind, picked out by a uniquely identifying description, which would be brought about by virtue of the laws of nature if some earlier event of a specified kind, picked out by uniquely identifying description, had happened at some earlier period of time — as dated by an actual event. Thus, one possible event is the first explosion which would have happened if I had lit a certain fuse with a certain set-up at the same time as a certain man walked out of the door. Or another possible event is the minute hand of this clock pointing to '12' for the second time if I had started the clock going when John started to run the race.[40]

Thus in terms of, or with reference to, causally related events we can distinguish or pick out different periods of time.

Be that as it may, the problem is this — Once God chooses to create time He can no longer be said to be omnipotent. For, the created time will consist of such different periods of time as past, present and future. And since past time is the time which is marked out by events that are not causally alterable God will have no power or control over past or events of the past time. Similarly though the events of future time and so far the future time itself would be causally affectible yet, they would not be future if they were perceptible. And if God could not perceive but say could infer them only, as we can do, then He could not be omniscient. In short, an everlasting

40. R. Swinburne, "God and Time" in Mohapatra et al. (eds.), (1992), p. 47.

God may not foresee future and about the past He cannot do anything. Even so far as He can know the past His knowledge would be a case of memory and not perception. God's perception will be confined to only the present. This would interfere with God's omniscience and omnipotence. God would have no control over time, which would run its course any way and God would be the sufferer. He would lose items of knowledge and also His immutability. He would have a time, which was lost and a future to attain. In addition His past will get ever lengthier and the number of items of knowledge that are lost will always increase. This shows that the Christian conception of God is not self-consistent. Earlier we saw that it was incompatible with cosmology and now we see it is not self-consistent either.

To sum up, many seem to believe that modern cosmology has nothing in it that is not compatible with Christianity. To be more precise it is sometimes believed that just as science does not deny that God has created the universe so also it seems to leave the scope for the divine intervention in the creation of the universe. For, it is the task of a scientific theory of the universe as a whole to identify some physical necessity why the universe comes to begin at all, why it begins precisely at that particular time when it begins and why it evolves in a particular way — say, in the way it has so far evolved up to the point when men could ask the questions we are discussing here. Many will think, following the suggestion made by Hawking, that if any theology admits that God freely chose to create the universe when the physical necessity or condition identified by science obtained, then there need not be any clash between science and (Christian) religion. It is reported that the Catholic Church has also announced that modern scientific cosmology is in line with the Christian theological account of the universe. We will not go into the motive behind such compatibility claim either from the side of science or from the side of the Church. But we will examine if the claim is correct. Two things are obvious. Christianity admits that the universe is created and hence has a beginning and also that God is the creator of this universe and of time. Cosmology under discussion here also admits that the universe has a beginning and does not feel any need to say that God could not have created this universe at the big-bang singularity.

However, the Christian God is omnipotent and eternal. But it seems that according to the Christian theology He could not be omnipotent if He were to create the universe only when the physical condition identified by cosmology obtained. An omnipotent Being would create freely. True, He might have freely chosen to create the universe at the big-bang, the physical condition identified by science. But also He might have chosen not to create at that point but at some other point or chosen never to create. This is simply not acceptable or meaningful in cosmology. Secondly, God might not have chosen to create time and this universe in time. But insofar as He has chosen to do so He had implicated Himself in temporality risking His eternity or immutability, omniscience and omnipotence — everything.

Swinburne thinks that still there is a way to argue that God's eternity, omniscience, etc. are all safe. We simply need, he appears to think, to take God's freedom seriously. This freedom is a part of his omniscience. It is He who, by His free choice, has created the universe, the time and also the events and thereby periods of time. These are among the things in terms of which we formulated our arguments against His eternity, omnipotence and so on. He might not simply have chosen to create this universe in which case arguments against His immutability, etc. could not even be formulated. To put the whole matter differently, the question is if God in Himself is unaffected by time under any assignable condition and under any interpretation of time (such as time before creation of the universe), does His eternity or the other properties in question get affected by time when it is created along with or after the creation of the universe? Swinburne thinks it does not. For even according to the objector time (measurable or distinguishable time) will affect Him only if and when it is there. It might not have been there. It, as a matter of fact, is because He freely chose to create time. So He cannot be said to be a prisoner of time. A prisoner does not have a choice to be or not to be a prisoner. God remains as much the Lord of time and free after His creation of the universe and time as He was before creation. In other words, even if He creates and thereby allows Him to be affected by temporality He is still the Lord and not the prisoner; for, He freely chooses to be affected by time and temporality. Is this argument sound or, let us ask, convincing? It sounds like saying that by committing suicide one proves that he was the master of his life. The fact is that he loses his life nonetheless. Similarly one can say that God loses His independence and omnipotence nonetheless once He chooses to create the world and along with it time.

We would like to note that Swinburne does not develop his, or Christian theory's view of the time that is not created and is there all the time including the time before the creation of the universe. Our cosmologist does not have any use of such a time and cuts it out of physics. But does Swinburne or Christianity have any use for it either? The only thing that he tells us is that before creation time would not have distinguishable periods like past, present and future. It is obviously so if we use these terms in the way explained. But what would be the answer to the simple and straightforward questions: was there a time before creation? Will it be inconsistent in Christianity to admit such a time? If such a time is there then what is the relation of this time to the other time — the created time? What would be God's relation to such a time? It seems to be assumed that whatever may be answer to other questions, God's relation to such a time would not make him mutable since this time does not change[41] or it would have periods of time. One may not still be convinced. Is it that there was no period division before creation or is it that we do not have any means of knowing if such divisions were there? Our not having the means of distinguishing or knowing the distinctions does not prove that the distinctions were not or could not have been there. All that Swinburne has shown is that there were no events before the universe was created and hence there was no means for us to distinguish periods of time before creation as we have now after the creation. So there could still be distinction to be drawn or known in some other way. Let us think in this way, God has created the universe at a point when He freely chose to do that. So one may conclude that before that point time was marked by the absence of God's choice to create (or better His wish to create); the next period of time is marked by God's choosing to create. So could we or could we not say that the time before creation would still have two periods, the period that ended when God wished to create the[42] universe and the period that follows His wishing to create (or the creation of the universe, assuming that there was not any or much time

41. Lot of discussion is there about this problematic but familiar way of speaking about time. See for example, J.J.C. Smart, "The River of Time" in A. Flew (ed.), *Essays in Conceptual Analysis* (New York: Macmillan, 1966), pp. 213-27.

42. This also is an important point why the universe and not this universe? Why Christianity does not admit that there were or could be more than one creation?

lapse between his wishing to create and the creation). If on the basis of such considerations we admit that there was not only a time before creation but also period division in that time then the earlier questions have to be answered in a way that does not turn Christian system of thought further inconsistent.

IV

A Philosophical Cosmology

We tried to show above that the Christian theory of the universe and time is incompatible with modern scientific cosmology and in addition, self-inconsistent. The features of the theory that particularly came for our discussion include belief in a creator God who is eternal besides being omnipotent, etc. and the belief that time, at least, measurable time, has a beginning. It is interesting to note that there is another theory of time and universe which includes all these features but which, to our mind, is both self-consistent and compatible with cosmology, at least, not incompatible for the same reasons for which Christianity was found incompatible. This situation itself should make a close discussion of this system of thought theoretically exciting. One can foresee that this system understands or interprets differently the otherwise same concepts, including the concepts involved in our discussion so far. This system of thought developed in India and is known as the Nyāya system of thought.[43] It is one of

43. We prefer to use the expression the Nyāya system of thought rather than the more widely used description the Nyāya School of *philosophy*. For the English word philosophy when used without qualification recalls many associations that do not hold good in case of Nyāya. At the same time we have no scope here to explain the differences of Nyāya "philosophy" with the standard systems of philosophy that developed in the West. For example, the contrast with science that is included among the normal →

the most technical and rigorously argued theoretical systems that the world has ever produced and which has a history of continuous development from, at least, the first century till today.[44] Unfortunately, we cannot help overlooking here most of its beautiful sophistications that are immensely theoretically useful, and also many rigorous analyses and formulations for which equal number of scholars seem to adore and dread it.

We would not only state the relevant doctrines of Nyāya in a rather non-technical way but also inquire if this theory is sound. If it turns out to be sound, then the Christian theory will lose, at least, its theoretical necessity. If on the other hand it can be shown that the Nyāya theory, besides being self-consistent, does better justice to our experience and usages, then it must be admitted to be a stronger theory. We find that on this count at least the Nyāya theory is better than both the Christian theology and scientific cosmology.[45] At this point one may ask the question, do we need a philosophical theory

→ associations of the term philosophy in modern English language does not have its strict parallel in India. Nyāya conducts thorough study of the physical nature including the origin of the physical universe, though as subservient to spiritual and soteriological quest for saving knowledge and freedom. Be that as it may there is here thorough analysis of many physical and mathematical concepts as well as both qualitative and quantitative concepts.

44. Though some modern scholars think that the system emerged in the first century great scholars of the subject like Mahamohopadhyay Phanibhusan Tarkavagisha dated it much earlier. See the Introduction of his first volume of *Nyāyadarśana* (in Bengali), 2nd edn.

45. There may be and are many other counts on which modern cosmology is far superior. What we emphasize is that there is need for a theory, which would be true not only to observations, in the narrow sense, but also to the established usages as well as the overall world-view with its social institutions and systems of values.

of creation when we now have a scientific theory of the same. The fact that we rarely, if at all, ask the alternative question, do we need a scientific theory of creation (or for the matter that of anything) when we have a philosophical theory of it, shows that we decide a priori that scientific theory is superior. We would argue that a philosophical theory or explanation could be as good as a scientific theory or explanation. Besides, the modern distinction between scientific and philosophical theory does not easily apply to classical theories of different cultures, not certainly of Indian culture.

We have seen reasons why the Christian doctrine is not compatible with cosmology. But those who are, otherwise, disposed to believing that the Christian doctrine of creation is compatible with scientific cosmology might think that since the Nyāya theory is incompatible with the Christian theory it should be somehow incompatible with scientific cosmology also. It may be profitable for us to note how much compatibility or incompatibility Nyāya has with cosmology or with the Christian theology. First, Nyāya has no difficulty in admitting that God creates this universe under certain conditions or when certain physical necessity like the big-bang obtains.[46] Similarly it can admit a number of other points also. One may, however, wonder how it can even be suggested that Nyāya is a parallel

---

46. The notion of big-bang is certainly not known before. But a modern Naiyāyika who knows about modern cosmology would not have in principle much difficulty in accepting or accommodating in his system of thought many important parts of this new cosmology. For example, since unlike Christianity, Nyāya does not believe in absolute creation and believes that God creates only when all the necessary conditions other than his own will are also there, there would be no difficulty in admitting that God creates only when necessary physical condition obtains. It is a different matter and matter of detail whether this condition is big-bang.

system of thought and not incompatible with cosmology when according to Nyāya time is eternal. We will find an answer to this later. For the present let us admit that for good philosophical reasons Nyāya admits that time is eternal. This part of Nyāya is hard to reconcile with what the Christian theology or modern cosmology teaches us. However, insofar as it admits that the universe has a beginning Nyāya is again compatible with both Christianity and cosmology. It is therefore clearly a third type of theory of the universe as a whole, i.e. of cosmology;[47] and it is quite natural that one would like to know more about this system and study it.

It is of particular interest to know why Nyāya says all those things that are, when taken together, apparently inconsistent. Is Nyāya a consistent system? Besides, even agreement in their theses alone does not make two systems compatible — for the reasons for saying those things may be quite different in the two systems so much so that the reasons of one system may be found unacceptable in the other. So it is also necessary to inquire whether the two theories in question are of the same type and follow the same norm or standard of rational acceptance. We would like to discuss these points, however briefly, a little later. For the present it suffices to note one interesting point. It is that even though Nyāya is a theistic system of thought, yet, unlike Christianity, its difference from cosmology will be informed more by logical requirement than by theological compulsion. Its arguments will be more philosophical rather than theological. And from a philosophical point of view and its analytical approach, it is of ultimate importance to analyse thoroughly and be clear about the concepts involved or being used in a certain inquiry. For example, in the context of our present inquiry into the

47. See Hawking (1988), p. 194.

subject of time that is studied in different disciplines, we cannot gain anything, not certainly the sort of gain we envisaged from such study — the theoretical understanding — if we are not clear about the senses in which expressions such as "time," "creation," "omnipotence," etc. are used in different systems in question. Those who do not pay the attention this point deserves often end up with cheap comparison and are sometimes found to argue at cross-purpose. People of other disciplines often misunderstand the characteristically philosophical insistence on more analysis of relevant concepts than are carried out in other theoretical systems as unnecessary and unproductive fastidiousness. Those who have practised it seriously and sincerely down the ages know how such analysis is both interesting and theoretically useful. In the Indian classical culture, at least that part of it which is called the theoretical culture, theories are marked by their argumentative and analytical character[48] no matter whether the subject matter of the theory in question is religion or medicine or even rituals, statecraft or aesthetics. Anyway, a

48. One may be reminded that the 2005 publication of Amartya Sen has the title *The Argumentative Indian*. He has rightly emphasized in that book that this more rationalistic, argumentative and analytical side of the Indian culture has not received the attention it deserves. See particularly the essay no. 7 of that book. For a detailed discussion of this point please see Mukhopadhyay, "The History of Science and Two Metamorphoses of Mind" in D.P. Chattopadhyaya et al. (eds.), *Language, Logic and Science in India* (New Delhi: A Project of Indian Science Philosophy and Culture publication, 1995). Many scholars refer to one statement of Manu to show how far Indians can go in the matter of emphasizing the importance of rationality. Manu said in connection with scriptural duty (*dharma*) that he alone knows *dharma* (which is generally thought to defy rational content or justification) who approaches it analytically and argumentatively and not others. I would also like to refer to the twentieth century works on *Arthaśāstra* by Panditraj Rajeswar Sastri Dravid.

Naiyāyika would like to inquire first if there is anything in the notion of time that makes it impossible for time to be eternal and not have a beginning or that there could be only one time and not many? If there is a time that has a beginning does it follow that God has created it or that it is real? Is there anything in the notion of creation that it has to be absolute creation in the Christian sense of the term? Is there anything in the notion of omnipotence that an omnipotent creator cannot be said to create only when a certain physical necessity or condition is there? Is there anything in the notion of a good argument that we can have such argument in science only? We would try to find out Nyāya answers to these questions.

In India there are many systems of thought, such as Buddhism, that do not admit the reality of time. But it is admitted on all hands that our everyday as well as theoretical language is replete with words that somehow involve reference to time or use temporal words. The systems that do not admit the reality of time also feel obliged to provide a good explanation — though not justification since that is not possible on the view that time is not real — of these usages. Those who, on the other hand admit time to be an item of reality, justify the usages in question by pointing at the fact that the experience that these usages have behind them is incontrovertible. However, as could be naturally expected, those who do not admit the reality of time have disputed this claim. But there is no dispute about the fact that usages in question are there and every theory is under obligation to offer or cite, if and when challenged, some good explanation (self-developed or borrowed) of this fact that would also be consistent with their theory. But to provide good explanation of a certain group of usages seems to be the primary task of the disciplines of language study such as linguistics, semantics, etc. Every Indian system of thought normally presupposes the account of language and usages of different kinds of words that has been given in the Pāṇinian system of linguistics. Occasionally systems like Nyāya or Bauddha feel compelled to resort to alternative accounts of, not language or words as such but, some portions or expressions of language. Nyāya, which is especially committed to analyzing theoretical and natural concepts, keeps behind its philosophical theory of time, the findings of linguistics regarding the usages in question. It should not be presumed however that these linguists are all aligned with the Nyāya metaphysics or ontology. Nor does the Nyāya system of thought accept what is known as the ontology or metaphysics of these linguists. In general these linguists are not realists as the Naiyāyikas are.[49] However, the summary account of time provided below is based to a great extent on literature on linguistics and the systems of Nyāya and Vaiśeṣika.

Time is what common men or even scientists hardly can do without and yet it is very difficult to say that they know in any precise sense what time is. They can hardly define it. In science we make do quite well with time. But science is not really of much help when one wants to be clear about the idea of time. Either they do not define it[50] or the accounts they offer do not fulfil the need for a precise definition. These do not satisfy fully the scientists themselves and philosophers are not satisfied either.

Motion is the basic subject of study of all physics.[51] An

49. This is not to deny that in their exhaustive treatment of the subject of time some *vyākaraṇa* included authentic summary of the Nyāya position in the matter. See particularly *Kālasamuddeśa* section of Bhartṛharis's *Vākyapadīyam*.

50. Incidentally the Glossary appended to Hawking's *A Brief History of Time* does not include time as one of it entries.

51. Cf. R.P. Feynman, *The Feynman Lectures on Physics*, vol. 1 (Narosa Publishing House, rpt. 1995), p. 51.

understanding of motion seems to involve reference to both time and space.[52] And yet physics has no very precise notion of time. It seems a scandal.[53] Philosophy seems to be in a better position. But there is a great difference between philosophy that has come down to us from long past and cosmology that started its career only in the later part of the twentieth century. The difference is that science wants to arrive at quantitative relationships between phenomena on the basis of quantitative observations. The study of time carried out by the Greeks, say, was philosophical; it was based on arguments that could be thought up in one's head.[54] This may be true as far as it goes but it does not go very far. For much of modern scientific cosmology is really in the head.[55] And we are discussing time in the context of cosmology.

Modern scientific work on time started when Galileo first measured time by observing (and noting carefully the results thereof) the behaviour of a ball that was allowed to roll down an inclined plane. If this is any indication then science is interested in measuring time and not defining it. Science also insists on clarity and precision. But it takes a concept to be sufficiently clear if we can carry out relevant measurements. And the history of the development of newer and newer

52. One may ask why time or anything else cannot move in time alone. From the point of view of Nyāya there is a very good answer. First, we meet very often with passages in which time is said to move. Flow of time is one such usage. But this is all metaphor (see J.J.C. Smart). For a Naiyāyika, time cannot move because it is infinite and only finite substances can have movement. And there is not a single substance, which is finite and exists only in time and does not have a position in space also.

53. This sometimes happens. Philosophers say philosophy has its own scandal. See M. Dummett, *Frege: Philosophy of Language* (Duckworth, 1992).

54. Feynman, op. cit., p. 50.

55. Cf. Hawking (1988) Acknowledgements, p. vii.

techniques of measuring time shows how insistent the scientists are on precision. So instead of making wrong demands it is wise to accept that what definition is to a philosopher measurement is to a scientist. At the same time the scientists should not misunderstand one who asks honestly, though not very wisely, at this stage perhaps, how is it possible to do anything definite to a thing if we do not understand what the thing is; how can we measure time without knowing what time is. And we cannot know a thing theoretically if we cannot define it. If so press a scientist can do hardly anything more than saying, "well Webster has failed to give us a good, non-circular, definition of time and if I say "Time is what happens when nothing else happens," that also doesn't get us very far. Maybe it is just as well if we *face the fact that time is one of the things we probably cannot define* (in the dictionary sense), and just say that it is what we already know it to be."[56] This confession along with what is said above leads one to think that for a scientist time is nothing but the measurement of it. If this is too hard to swallow, though it is a more accurate way of putting the matter, then time means in science measured or at least measurable time.

History tells us that philosophers did not need to be told by the scientists that it was very difficult to find an acceptable definition of time; for that much they had discovered long before.[57] With their remarkable practical sense the theoreticians in the field of science, however, did not allow themselves to get stuck at this. They went on with the hard facts of the matter, namely, measurements of time. Did the philosophers have any such hard facts of the matter with which they could begin or continue their inquiry of time? The answer to this is definitely known today as much as it was known

56. Feynman et al., p. 51, emphasis added.

57. Augustine clearly stated that in his *Confessions*.

before. And the answer has nothing technical about it. The hard facts of the matter are human usages. And the question which must bother anyone with a theoretical bent of mind is, can we make good sense of or consistent theory on our use of words like "time," "past," "present" and so on? One may find here the beginning of philosophy as opposed to science for the question to be addressed here relates to sense or meaning as distinct from fact. It is one of the usual ways of distinguishing science from philosophy to say that the former is a factual study and the latter a conceptual study. Be that as it may, even scientists sometimes cannot avoid raising questions about meaning. "It is now believed that at least our part of the universe had its beginning about ten or twelve billion years ago. We do not know what happened before then. In fact, we may well ask again: does the question make any *sense*? Does an earlier time have any *meaning*?"[58]

We said above that it is a primary objective of linguistics in India to build a consistent theory and good explanation of our common (and non-common) usages about time. One should not conclude hastily that Indian mind never addressed the question of measuring time.[59] To return to our point it would be in order to search if and what light the linguists can

58. Feynman, p. 55. Emphasis added. A scientist would, however, like to qualify the question by adding "at the present state of our knowledge?"

59. Indian mind addressed the linguistic question of meaning of relevant words but also the more scientific questions about measurement of time. In his paper "Physico-Chemical Ideas in ancient and Medieval India" Chanchal Kumar Majumdar, one of the best recognized physicists of India, admired for his talent, sweep of scholarship and accuracy of presentation, writes, "How was time measured? On the large scale, the year was determined very accurately by Indian astronomers. . . . Indian astronomers estimated one "yuga" as 43,20,000 years. . . . Their estimate has been acknowledged to be remarkable. On the smaller scale . . .

→

shed on our problem. The earliest among the most celebrated works in this field is a 500 BCE work by Pāṇini. He has a *sūtra* (aphorism), which reads *kālaḥ parimāṇinā*.[60] It is one of the earliest *sūtras* of Pāṇini where some profound insight regarding time or uses of temporal words has been expressed. Commentators[61] have discussed the *sūtra* at great length. We would note some of the important suggestions that one can derive from reading this *sūtra* and later elucidations of it. The word *kāla* (time) does not mean (temporal) measure but other temporal words do. So we cannot afford to miss that the logic of "time" is different from that of words like "past," "present," "month," "year," etc. in such expressions as "one month old" or "one year old." Besides, having its own interest, especially as it leads to clarifying what it means to be a measurable time, the discussion is one of the earliest records where a distinction between time and measurable time has been adumbrated. There are many more interesting discussions on various aspects of time throughout Pāṇini's work in question, which have been later on taken up and considered in different philosophical schools of India. It is extremely unfortunate that we cannot take account of many such beautiful discussions on intricate issues relating to time that one can find without much difficulty in the literature of Nyāya (and some other philosophical systems as well) and linguistics. We indicate very briefly one or two relevant points from Nyāya system of thought.

The word time has been used in many different senses in literary works. Again, sometimes it is difficult for outsiders

→ the accuracy was limited." In the Journal, *Science Philosophy Interface*, vol. 5, no. 1, 2000.

60. Pāṇini, *Aṣṭādhyāyī* 2.2.5.

61. Such as Kaiyaṭa, etc.

to believe that one is not talking figuratively when one says that time is not different from God.[62] Anyway, Naiyāikas find good reasons for using the word time at least in two different senses. What unites the two senses is that the word time signifies a certain magnitude in that it primarily signifies what has this magnitude. The same holds for space. In the spatial realm things are distinguished as having shortest extension, or shorter extension and maximum extension. Like spatial magnitude or extension temporal magnitude or duration also characterizes things. As one of the twenty-four types of quality, magnitude (*parimāṇa*) must inhere in some substance. No substance can fail to have magnitude (spatial or temporal). A substance that exists wherever any substance (other than the type of things space and time are) in the universe exists is said to have infinite magnitude (*vibhū parimāṇa*) — whether spatial or temporal. In other words a substance that stands related to (by way of conjunction) every substance of the universe that has motion (*mūrtta*) has infinite magnitude. Now substances are also divided into two categories: those that have as their essential possession only one (type of) sensible quality (which quality is amenable to only one type of sense organ) and those that have none. Of the nine substances enumerated in the Nyāya-Vaiśeṣika scheme of ontology only three lack such sensible quality (*viśeṣa guṇa*). Of these three only two have infinite magnitude. One is time or *kāla* and the other is *dik* or roughly space.[63] Spatial distinctions like "near"

62. Note that the same thing has been said in the *Bhagavad-Gītā* and in a technical work of the Nyāya school by Raghunatha Siromani who is known as one of the most astute thinkers the country has ever produced.

63. According to Nyāya both these are used as having direction. However, in themselves, that is independent of reference to our conceptual framework, they do not have any distinguishable directions.

and "far" bear reference to *dik* or space and temporal distinctions as "younger" and "older" bear reference to time or *kāla*. So far *kāla* or time is a substance to which reference has to be made whenever we are to assign any measurable temporal duration to anything (any substance). There is no circularity in this account because time itself is not a temporal duration. It is indeed a substance and like all other substances it has magnitude. Further, its magnitude is infinite. True, but this infinite magnitude does not mean infinite duration (just as in case of space it does not mean infinite extension). Infinitude has been so defined above as to make no reference to extension or duration though it makes reference to conjunction with other substances. Such a definition of magnitude is common to both time and space. So far in this first sense time is a substance, which is ubiquitous. Its infinity is not a measurable quantity involving addition say of infinite units of time. (Till now we have given no sense to the expression "unit of time.") This one ubiquitous time is indivisible and hence has no parts. This time is further absolute *eternal* and universal receptacle (*jagadādhāra*).

There is another sort of time or temporal magnitude clue to which is provided by verb words in a language, or more precisely by the fact that these words admit of conjugational variations. Different tenses of verb words show that there are periods of time such as past, present and future which comc primarily as modifier of verbs. So far then time in the sense of temporal period is temporal determination of the meaning of verb words, i.e. actions or occurrences of events. Insofar as the words past, present and future refer to some periods of time they refer to time that is relative, impermanent and measurable, as measurable time is either a unit of time or sum of a number of units of time. Ordinary ways of clarifying the senses of impermanent times or, say past, present, etc. can hardly do. It will not do to say that the past is that which we remember and the present is that which we perceive. For, we can also perceive the past. This is precisely the case when we see today the state of a distant star from which it takes years for light rays to reach the earth. For the same reason we cannot give much importance to what we were given to understand to be a more scientific and sophisticated account of past, present and future in terms of what we can or cannot do to certain particular events.[64] Nyāya has given us a very sophisticated and precise account of all these with reference to the motion of the sun.[65] There may be the problem of how far we can generalize such an account. All these fall beyond the purview of the present discussion. We just note here that there are two times, one permanent and the other impermanent.[66]

One benefit of admitting a time that does not have a period division in it is that we can avoid the usual charge that one

64. We can think of counter examples to what was claimed above to be more scientifically acceptable account of periods of time and hence of the corresponding words. For, we can do something to events in the past. Suppose certain events in the past would have otherwise produced a certain effect. But we can do something so that such effect could never be produced. It is in this way we can interfere with the past event or its very nature.

65. This is the literal translation of the Saṁskṛta expression used, viz. *ādityagati*.

66. While talking of impermanence normally the authors speak of particular periods of time. For in the Aghamarṣana-Sūkta of the *Ṛgveda* we hear of the creation of the days and nights and of years. Similarly in the passages like *pratyayanti punargatanadivasa* we hear of destruction of days. Great periods of time like *kalpa* and *manvantara* are all measurable times and they are measured in terms of years that have beginning and end. But the creation or impermanence of *kāla* as such is rarely spoken of. See, however, *Vāyupurāṇam* and the *Gurugītā*.

who admits measurable time and distinctions of past, present, etc. places himself under the compulsion of admitting infinite number of times, i.e. one is involved in infinite regress. The Nyāya view of the eternity of this one time is based on the two characteristics of it, namely, its being a substance and having no parts. Anything that is a substance and is indivisible can have no beginning and no destruction. Is there any observable evidence? We have never observed any substance, which satisfies this description: not having a beginning or an end. But we have strong arguments based on observable facts of established usages involving temporal words and our incontrovertible experience behind these usages. Another important point to note is that this Time (let us use capital T for this eternal and single time) is an item of reality. It is one of the nine items enumerated under the first of the nine categories of reality by the Vaiśeṣikas.

To recapitulate, the hard observable facts of the matter, which for philosophers are both a testing ground for their theory and one of the phenomena which the theory is to organize and explain, are the usages involving temporal words or time-words. Of these the word "time" does not really mean magnitude whereas other such words like days and months, etc. do. For one thing, time itself cannot be used to measure relative temporal duration of any event. So it would not be right to say that time is a time-word where such words are expressive of measurable magnitude. The reason why time cannot be used for measuring duration is that it is unlimited. Only things having limit can be used to measure and thereby determine quantity.[67] Unlimited space is not and cannot be used to measure relative spatial distance. We use a meter scale,

67. Cf. Panini 2.2.5 and explanations on it including the explanation of Kaiyaṭa.

or a meter rod, which is a limited thing to measure the relative distance of things in space. Similarly we use day and month to measure the relative span of life of things in time as when we say a day-old baby or one-year-old building. But by units like day or moment we measure relative distance of events that are already in time. This is what we mean by measuring relative duration. Measuring time means measuring relative duration, span, life, of events *in time*. We say this boy is older than that boy, or this boy is older when compared to the other boy, meaning thereby that this boy has lived longer, had a longer life than the life of the other boy? How longer is the life of this boy relative to the life of that boy? Well, we say so many days or months and so on. So we measure by using an unit of measurement, say day; we measure the relative duration of events like life in time or life of things in time. Here we use two words time and day. Day is time in the sense that it is a part of time, which in its turn means that it is used to measure duration of things in Time. What is this Time in which we measure the relative duration of events with the help of the temporal unit, say, day? This is not a totality of days and months. Such totality of days or if you like of seconds or *kṣaṇa*s may be of short or large duration but even the largest span we get in this way would be limited. It would be a measurable unit of duration however large. As such it can, in principle, be used to measure the relative duration of events in Time. So we can never reduce this Time into days or months or whatever units of time we use or their multiples. It comes to this that days and months that are known as periods of time are not Time in the sense in which those events, the relative duration of which we measure in terms of days and months, exist or occur. A day is a certain section of movement of the earth rotating around the sun, or what comes to the same thing, a certain section of the movement of the sun (*ādityagati*) as we observe from the earth. We use this limited span of the movement of the sun as both itself a measured and measurable time and unit of measuring the relative span of events in Time.

To make it short,[68] we identify or take one part of the four-part atomic action or motion — be that the action that is called the batting of the eyelids or movement of a ball from one point in space to the next adjacent point in it — and call it the *unit* or smallest *part of time*, a moment (of time) or one (*eka*) *kṣaṇa*. With this or with a larger period of time (such as a day or year) that is the sum of some finite number of *kṣaṇa*s, we measure the relative span or duration of events in Time. This time, such as a day or a month, is nothing but action or motion (*kriyā*) or part or sum thereof, but it is still called time only in a derivative sense of being the measure of time. To put it differently, ontologically or in reality there is only one Time. Our usages about different times or periods of time force us to admit that one Time is *used as different* times (actually, periods of Time artificially created by convention) when taken as qualified by or related to different limiting things. For example, one single space is referred to as different spaces — space covered by this room and space covered by that room. Actually the rooms are different and not the space. Space is only used as different when taken in relation to different sets of walls that enclose space. Similarly Time is only used as different when taken in relation to such limited things as action or motion that has beginning and end. It should not be asked, well, since we can make do with days and months, etc., why posit one extra entity called Time? We have partially answered it. Without admitting it we cannot make

68. For details and technical formulations one should consult the original texts of Nyāya Vaiśeṣika literature.

sense of that part of our usages, which involve reference to relative duration of events in Time. There is another explanation, a causal explanation, also. This explanation also bears reference to our usages. It says in effect that we have to admit Time as (one of the) causes of such usages as simultaneous, earlier, later and so on. We cannot explain these usages, as may be thought possible otherwise, in terms of say the motion of the sun, in the sense explained — for the sun or the motion of the sun is not in direct contact with the events the relative span of which we measure. But both the sun and its movement on the one hand and the events, the relative duration between which is being measured, on the other, are *in Time* and hence, through Time only the necessary relationship between them is established without which there could not be the relation of cause and effect between them and as a result we could not explain the usages in question.

The important point for us is that Nyāya admits two sorts of time, one, a real and uncreated Time and a second one that has a beginning and is a sort of imaginary time (*kalpita* or *kriyopalakṣita kāla*). This second time is the measurable time and it is also created. But it is we who create it by creating the necessary convention as explained above. In cosmology also one sometimes finds reference to both a real and an imaginary time to which we do not relate the Nyāya division at the moment. We have no time now to discuss here the cosmologist's sense of imaginary and real time and without that we cannot say how if at all the Nyāya division of time can be related to that. But cosmologist's sense is as technical as the Naiyāika's sense.

The other relevant concepts that we need to clarify include creation. In the Nyāya system of thought creation necessarily means creation in time and hence in Time. Actually, Nyāya insists that in standard usage no sense is given to creation, which is not creation in time or Time. This system not only uses creation in this sense but also takes upon itself the task of providing necessary theoretical support to this usage. The point is that creation of a thing means that thing's coming into contact with (pre-existing) Time and time (for convenience henceforward we would use the spelling time unless it is absolutely necessary to refer to Time exclusively). It is not possible for a thing to come in contact with time later than when it is produced. This obviously applies to things that have a beginning. For the things that are eternal, either in the sense of time transcending or in the sense of everlasting in time, it is not possible that there could be a period or point of time prior to or later than this eternal thing — for whereas time has a beginning when it begins it begins by getting connected with the eternal thing, which is already there. This means the existence of eternal thing has a non-temporal sense. And for the sake of generality and uniformity of usages a Naiyāyika does not give a temporal sense to existence. To be more precise the word existence is used in two different senses. We sometimes use it to mean the real. What exists is real. But the converse is not true. To be real a thing does not need to exist; if exists means "exists in time" — though this latter sense would not apply to time itself. For a thing to be real it must have being (*sattā*). Such a real thing may or may not have a beginning. Those which have being, come to be or have *sattā* only when they are produced or created. And anything that is created or produced is created or produced in time. More particularly, it is created in a certain point in time; it is not everlasting in time. The thing's coming into contact, this event, is itself as occurrent as the thing itself. The first contact with time coincides with the production of the thing. So production or the beginning is this first (from the point of view of the history of the thing in question) contact with time, whereas this point of time is marked out as the point succeeding the point at which the thing's absence existing so long comes to an end. The actual formulation is more technical and precise.[69] Our point here is that creation means to come in contact with a time that is already there. So when cosmology says that there was no time when the universe was created but time came to be along with or slightly later than the creation of the universe, the use of creation is non-standard to say the least. There is in principle no objection to using a word in a new sense but that sense has to be clearly stated. In this regard both cosmology and Christian theology seem to be deficient or at least not thoroughgoing or fully analytic.

We have said earlier that it is also a very strong point in favour of the Nyāya account of time that it is free from, because it admits two kinds of time, the usual problem that the philosophers point out against the conception of time (actually measurable time) that it is vitiated by infinite regress. Now we pass over to the other aspect of the standard notion of creation, which again seems to be violated by both cosmology and the Christian theology. First, the creation of a created thing cannot be its natural property. What is meant is that if any property is the natural possession of a thing then that thing would have the property in any case and all the time; its possession would not be relative to anything. But if the creation of thing were in this sense unconditional then it would be always there and hence uncreated. In some sense or other there is recognition of this point both in cosmology and in Christianity. Cosmology admits a physical condition or necessity, infinite density of matter (!), say, that "led" to the big-bang or the beginning of the universe. The Christianity

69. See for example Panchanan Sastri's translation and elucidation (in Bengali) of Annambhatta, *Tarkasaṁgraha* with *Dīpikā*, p. 68.

would say that prior to the beginning of the universe and as the cause of it there was God and His freedom, omniscience, etc. But this will not do. Any creation is a causal creation. The created thing comes to be and be connected to time due to some *pre-existing* cause. A reflection will convince anyone that if existence depended solely on some pre-existing cause that was eternal or that was itself created then the creation of the thing in question could not be explained theoretically. The point has been discussed in great detail in Nyāya texts.[70] The conclusion is that the set of causal conditions of the universe (or for that matter anything) must include at least one factor that is itself not created and at least one other condition that is itself created. As a matter of fact, to be absolutely brief, in the Nyāya account of the beginning of the universe, God creates the universe in Time by using and utilizing certain pre-existing factors some of which are eternal and some non-eternal. This makes the Nyāya creation of the universe creation under physical necessity. It also solves the problem of how the universe can be created at a single point of time since the whole of the universe is not given at one point; in fact so many things are still happening and being created making the universe grow. For Nyāya, creation of the universe means creation of the first and simplest of composite matter, called dyad. This dyad is created by joining, so to say, two elementary particles[71] of matter. At this point God's intervention was necessary. For the elementary particles could not get joined together or connected on their own; otherwise there could be composite matter always. This account has its analogue in

70. See Udayana's *Nyāyakusumāñjaliḥ* (cited earlier) chapter one.

71. These are not elementary particles in the sense of quantum mechanics, i.e. non-eternal units of matter into which atoms may be analysed. Elementary matter is here used in the sense of *paramāṇu* that is unit of matter that cannot be analysed in principle.

cosmology in that in cosmology we may say that the creation of the universe, which is never given in its totality, is the creation of the elementary particles of matter and the forces that combine them somehow.[72]

One more point before we close this section. Nyāya account of the beginning of the universe given above makes it amply clear that it is a sort of theological account, if you like; but it is importantly different from some other theological accounts such as we find in the Christianity. In it creation is not absolute, it is not creation out of nothing as seems to be the case, as we have shown above, with cosmology or Christian theology. This was one of the reasons why we remarked that in the Nyāya account logical necessity counts for more than theological compulsion. The result, some may think, is lack of clarity created by our compromising with the omnipotence of God. If God can create, as Nyāya is said to admit, only under extraneous conditions and necessities then how can God be omnipotent? Nyāya however does admit God to be omniscient and omnipotent as all do. The solution, it may be presumed, lies in the sense of the word in question. There seems to be a mystical sense and a rational and realistic sense of omniscience and omnipotence. The former contends that God or anything is omnipotent if and only if it can do everything. There should

72. Nyāya would find difficulty in accepting that the elementary particles are created unless we admit still simpler matter, say, *paramāṇu*, from which or combining which they are created. Besides Nyāya would find difficulty in accepting as final that the forces that are all very much material fully explains why at a particular point of time two elementary particles are related. May be Nyāya conducts its search at still deeper a level than cosmology which shows that these two explanations are two stages of explanations rather than two rival explanations. But we do not have enough evidence, rational or empirical to conclude this way or that.

not be anything in principle that God cannot create. This seems to be the Christian sense of the term. As it stands this account doesn't make sense. But what it actually means, and that is obvious, is that God has the power to create everything other than Himself. Why restrict the meaning of everything? The reason, it may be argued, is that God is eternal and uncreated. Nyāya would like to extend the argument and say first that God creates everything that is non-eternal — for it makes no sense to say that God creates something that is uncreated. It would be quickly pointed out, can God create everything that has a beginning? Possibly not, He cannot create the thing x that has already been created, say created by Him. So according to Nyāya the only thing that we can mean by God's omnipotence is His power to create everything that is logically possible to create. But this seems to be too restricted a sense. Even a man creates only what is logically possible — why then call God omnipotent? The Nyāya answer is this — there are two types of things altogether that are logically impossible to create: one that is always there in time and the other that can never be in any point or period of time. The example of the former kind of thing is God, Time, Space, human self[73] and the like. But "things" like square circle or rabbit's horn fall in the second category. Nyāya holds that things of none of these two categories can be created either by man or by God. Question of creation becomes meaningful with reference to things that form a third category. In this category also there are things such as the universe, which no one can conceivably manage to create. But since it is logically possible to create them it follows that there is a creator who can create things

73. In Christianity and in some systems of philosophy including a few Indian systems, human self is also created. But the majority and representative Indian view is that self whether human or divine is eternal.

that no one other than him can physically create. This is the Nyāya sense of omnipotence. Hence it does not matter even if God does not create everything so far as He *can* create physically everything that can be created logically. This description is uniquely satisfied by God alone. No one else can claim to be able to satisfy this description or He is God. Nyāya understands the predicate omniscience in the like manner; so no one can attribute to God the knowledge of the presence of a square circle, say. God is omniscient in the sense that He (alone) Knows and Knows actually and directly what can be logically known. Only things that are not self-contradictory like square circle fall into this category.

This is a very rough sketch of the Nyāya position in the matter in hand. This system of thought also presents us examples of arguments and explanations that are as good as one can find in science or, in the words of Swinburne, which are scientifically good without being scientific.[74] We believe that there is nothing wrong if one says that in a broad sense a rationally acceptable argument or explanation should be in line with the beliefs and practices in science. This is indeed so but not for the fact that science alone has the authority to detect what is rational but science itself pursues and exemplifies the rational mode of arguing and investigating which however is not confined to the researches in today's sciences or the Western mode of thinking alone. In this connection we may as well quote a passage from the writings of a great Indian mind —

> It has just been said that none of the so-called arguments or proofs for the existence of Theos in the Judaic-Christian

---

74. See, P.K. Mukhopadhyay, "Rationality and Religion", in Mohapatra et al. (eds.) *God, Time and Evil* (Bhubaneswar: Utkal University, 1992).

tradition can be claimed to be unexceptionable from a purely rational point of view, i.e. from a standpoint which relies only on ordinary perception and inference. In the *Vaidika* or Hindu tradition, however, there are at least four purely rational arguments which claim to establish the existence of some supreme spirit regulating the course of natural phenomena.[75]

V

The Fourth Arrow of time

In this section we propose to discuss time in relation to the ideology of progress. Modern scientific cosmology is not just any scientific theory such as the theory of light or of gravity and the like. It consciously aims at presenting us with a total picture of the universe[76] and in doing that it also takes seriously into consideration the creation and evolution of this earth and the existence in it of human beings like us who can raise and discuss questions about the origin of the universe. Indeed the works of Ptolemy on the one hand and of Copernicus, Galileo and Newton on the other resulted in the development of different world-views; yet it is doubtful whether they themselves wanted to offer different world-views. But some of the modern cosmologists today are consciously presenting us with a new picture of the universe with the world in it, which we inhabit. It may not be therefore completely out of place to inquire in which respects the new picture the cosmologists present today is likely to change — modify, replace or reinforce — the existing world-view. It is also quite

75. Gopinath Bhattacharya, "Theism and Antitheistic Theories in Indian Philosophy" in his *Essays in Analytical Philosophy* (Calcutta: Sanskrit Pustak Bhandar, 1989), pp. 173-88.

76. To be fair the cosmologist aspires to give us the total picture of the physical universe at the most. But we will ignore this point.

pertinent to ask whether they are aware of the implications or bearings of their suggested theory on the existing world-view. To put it differently, no scientific theory emerges in an intellectual or socio-cultural vacuum. So, by taking the word in a wider sense we would like to include among the observable data of a cosmological theory — which it is the task of a scientific theory to organize and explain and in terms of which, as predictable observational consequences of the theory, it is to be tested — not only the existence of human beings but also their beliefs and practices (or the people in question) and the way they behave or speak. So current and established usages and conceptual framework cannot be ignored if we want our theory to be empirical and not merely a priori. When we do so, however, we cannot but be a little alarmed at first to see that the theory in question destroys the very foundation of man's social existence. Though a little careful study may allay the fear by drawing our attention to certain technical elaboration of the theory, yet the effort would appear as more a sophistry than a serious reply from an empirical theory. So, if not practical yet theoretical uneasiness continues as we find that the cosmologist's reply is unconvincing.

The point at issue is this — theoreticians of different persuasions on the one hand and common men on the other all agree on one feature of time, that it has direction. It is therefore not just an abstract theorem of a formal theory. A belief in this feature has gone into determining so much of our views and practices, our language and thought that there would be total chaos if we are today asked to give up this belief. That does not mean that this idea of direction of time is very clear. But to try to clarify it is one thing and it is vastly a different thing if we are asked to give it up at the cost of changing, we do not know how, the entire world-view that we have. It is quite all right if it is said that in science we cannot, as scientists, understand what is 'direction of time' just as we cannot understand what 'spatial direction' is. They are more a matter of folk psychology than rigorous science. There is no scientific explanation of this feature of time. And in one's capacity as a scientist one does not know whether time really has a direction. One may suspect that current science does not have enough resources at present to distinguish between past and future. But it would be completely preposterous to ask us to give up our belief in the distinction between the past and the present or the present and the future. It is on record that many theoreticians discovered long back in linguistics,[77] philosophy[78] and so on that it is very difficult to make sense of the terms like present, past and the like. But they took upon them to provide a coherent theory of time, which would include some reasonable explanation of such usages and beliefs. Had it not been for this — such constraints to explain rather than explain away established habits of speech and actions — theory building would have been a very easy task and a completely a priori matter. No responsible theoretician, particularly in the field of empirical theories like the science of physics, would like to simply end the matter by saying that he as a scientist cannot

77. See Pāṇini's *sūtra* 2.2.5 and the commentaries on it. There are many other *sūtra*s in Pāṇini that deal with different aspects of time. We have discussed above from the Nyāya-Vaiśeṣika point of view the conventional nature of periods of time and hence by implication of the direction of time too. But that is a different matter.

78. Consult for example the basic text of classical Nyāya system of thought dating back from at least first century, particularly *sūtra*s 2.1.39-45 of *Nyāyadarśanam* by Gautama along with the commentaries on them. Also one can consult many standard texts and views of persons like Bradley, McTaggart, J.J.C. Smart and so on, to name a few randomly.

make any sense of direction of time. He would rather try to explain it in a way that would be consistent with the science he represents. We have fortunately such a scientist in Hawking. And his explanation can hardly be less than the best possible in the present state of our knowledge of our culture and science. But the result does seem at one end to be disastrous for our world-view and on the other it appears to be mere technicalities devoid of any substantive content.

Even up to the time of the Special theory of relativity the scientists worked with the conception of a static view of the universe and a notion of absolute time, which did not flatly contradict common views; at least no such implications were drawn. But since Friedman's prediction was confirmed by Hubble's observations, both as late as the first quarter of the twentieth century, the expanding model is widely used to understand and represent the universe. Since it is an expanding universe it must have started expanding at a certain point in the past. That time is called the big-bang. So the cosmological arrow of time has a definite direction, from the big-bang when the universe was infinitely small and dense to more and more expanded state. How does this arrow compare with our psychological arrow? It is difficult to say. Is the direction from the remembered past to the imaginable future the direction of the expansion of the universe from the very small to the ever larger? We would not repeat, what we said earlier, that the notions of past, present and the like are not very clear. But can we answer the question whether or not the psychological arrow and the cosmological arrow point in the same direction? An answer can be found if we can decide how each of these arrows stand in relation to another known and perhaps better understood arrow of time, namely the thermodynamic arrow of time. It also has a definite direction. It points to the direction in which entropy increases. If now it can be said that both the expansion of the universe and the movement from the past to the future involve a movement towards more and more disorder, that is, if the future is a more disordered state of knowledge or the universe, as the case may be, and the more the universe evolves or expands the more is the amount of disorder, then the desired correlation can be found. This has been argued to be the case. But before we complicate the situation by adding one more arrow of time, we note one of the two difficult points in the explanation. It has to be assumed that the expansion of the universe would be *for all practical purpose* endless, that is, there would not be after some time contraction of the universe. Of course, for this we have to admit that the universe would be and is expanding at a critical rate so that it just avoids collapse or re-collapse. So no-boundary condition and the critical rate of expansion have to be assumed of course on good grounds such as weak entropic principle. Before we turn to the other difficulty in this cosmological attempt to relate the three arrows, we want to introduce another arrow, a fourth arrow — call it the cultural arrow or the arrow of progress.

Every culture has its own idea of progress or own interpretation of this arrow of progress and it will be necessary for us to refer to some of these different ideas. However, in the context of our discussion of modern scientific cosmology and its thermodynamic and cosmological arrows, it would be more pertinent to discuss the idea and interpretation this arrow has in what is known as the secular and scientific culture of the modern West — for it has been said "no single idea has dominated Western civilization in modern times more than the idea of progress."[79] On the other hand, modern science is

79. Joseph Anthony Mazzeo, *Renaissance and Revolution: The Remaking of European Thought* (London: Methuen & Co Ltd, 1967), p. 275.

an integral part of this modern civilization or modern world-view, which is rightly described as the scientific world-view. Two things that are most prominently enshrined in this world-view are what may be called the ideology or utopia of progress and (modern) science. So it would be a little surprising, to say the least, if modern advances in science are found to be at odds with the ideology of progress — the dominant trend of the very culture within which it developed and which it helped to shape. To begin with, the idea of modern progress seems to be quite in line with the cosmological and thermodynamic arrows of time as much as it is in line with the theory of evolution (originally biological but later generalized into almost a whole world-view). For one thing, the modern idea of progress does not envisage any definite end of progress. The progress of man is indefinite and it has its counterpart in the cosmologist's view that does not envisage that the evolution of the universe or its expansion will stop or that there will be a reversal of this process. But let us first note how much the modern idea of progress is informed by modern science and scientific culture. This idea of progress is markedly different from, say, the ideas of progress we find in the Greek or Christian cultures. It expresses "the conviction that the process of social and cultural change we see about us are taking mankind in a desirable direction *in the long run*" and in spite of some possible minor setbacks man's otherwise steady *ascent* from his origins in barbarism to a golden future would *continue indefinitely*. This idea of progress or of cultural arrow is indeed very modern, almost contemporaneous with modern science. "The notion of gradual, continual progress, with no discernible limit, in a more or less linear ascent from an inferior condition, was unknown to mankind before the seventeenth century."[80]

---

80. Joseph Anthony Mazzeo, op. cit., p. 274.

It is different from the older Christian idea of progress in very many respects. According to Christianity human progress has a definite end but the golden (?) end is not in this temporal world, nor can it be attained by man's own effort or on the strength of his growing knowledge of nature. It will be available to select a few through God's grace. Modern idea of progress is very secular; it is understood as the improvement of man's condition in this world and by man's own effort. Every man can in principle attain his personal improvement or can contribute to collective socio-cultural progress through his own effort. By using his personal and natural capacities he can acquire knowledge, which is power enough to ensure desirable improvement. This knowledge again is not the saving knowledge to be had from religion or religious authority but from science. Science is knowledge and, in principle, any man can achieve it. Given this idea of progress, it would be a great shock if science turns out to devalue human achievements so far and predict that instead of improving indefinitely man is bound to lose all his achievements, which are signposts in the short history of progress of mankind according to the modern scientific and secular idea of progress. The Thermodynamic arrow of time seems to point to this direction. If the other two arrows are interpreted in the line of the thermodynamic arrow then all the three arrows will contradict the modern arrow of progress. If they are not so interpreted then there can be no uniform interpretation of the three arrows of time and the commonly accepted feature of time — its having a fixed direction — can hardly be reconcilable with science. But the cultural arrow of time, at least as it is understood in the modern scientific culture, implies the linear view of time. This linear time has its cultural counterpart in man's continual and indefinite progress, or potentiality for that.

Neither the Greek nor the Indian idea of progress on the other hand envisages that human progress is indefinite. In these ideas the goal of progress is also not indefinite. Though, however, the goal of progress in Greek culture is more secular and social than it is in Indian culture yet the Indian conception of the goal or end of human progress is different in important ways from the Christian idea of the same. Worldly prosperity including the improvement in social conditions (*abhyudaya*) is considered to be a great (if not the highest) and worthy pursuit. Further, in both these cultures great emphasis is placed on man's knowledge and his own effort as means for attaining progress and ultimately individual and collective fulfilment. Be that as it may the definite termination of human progress and the idea of cyclical time, in Greek and Indian culture, are opposed to modern European as well as scientific ideas of progress and time. However, in another respect the Indian culture and hence the Nyāya system of thought seems to be able to accommodate the modern cosmological conception of time and its implication. In these systems, as also in Greek culture, we find the presence of what is called eschatology myths.[81] Though theoretically speaking belief in cyclical change and a belief in periodical dissolution of the universe do go very well together, yet in Indian system of thought it takes incredibly long[82] years to reach even the state of dissolution just ahead in this cycle. So also, according to modern cosmology, the universe will be destroyed in principle but after such a long time and so long after mankind is destroyed that we can take the universe to be unending for all practical purposes. So only in this sense cosmology and its three arrows

81. In Indian culture they are much more than myth, but we will not pursue the point here.

82. P.V. Kane, *History of Dharmaśāstra*, vol. V, part I (1974), chapter XIX.

of time will not practically conflict with either the modern European or Indian idea of progress. And this leads us to the final consideration that we have in support of our view that the cosmological theory of time is inconsistent with the Indian as well as modern European world-views. Incidentally I would like to note, which I would have no scope to discuss here, two more features of the Indian conception of time that are very important in the context of progress. First, it is not so clear in Greek sources whether the Greeks admitted time to be eternal or even measurable time to be beginningless. But the view of the system of Nyāya, and it is a fairly representative view of Indian culture as a whole, is very definite and explicit. Nyāya admits that the past is unlimited though the future is limited. There is a definite termination of the development of the human world and man's culture or progress. The future or the human future and the human world are thus limited; it is not, as is claimed in the modern scientific culture of the West, indefinite or unlimited. Add to this belief in the finite and limited future of man and his progress the view, what is also quite clear in the Greek world-view, that the movement of time and civilization is cyclic, it follows that the grand finale is not an utopia, merely believed or imagined future state of being but a state realized in the past, perhaps many times. In the Greek or in Indian culture the belief in the golden and final state is more a racial and cultural memory than a wish or an imagination. While these two cultures as well as the modern Western culture are marked by man's aspiration towards a golden state yet people in the former two cultures are more assured of the success of their pursuit than the modern man can claim. The second feature of the Indian and the Nyāya view, which is markedly absent from the modern world-view, is that man's past is unlimited. Both the past of a single human individual as well as that of the collectivity called human race have no beginning. This point has been argued thoroughly in Nyāya system of thought but we cannot go into their arguments or the details of this aspect of their theory of the past. To just state their point in a sentence, they believe that there is an assignable beginning of the life of any given human individual or created universe. But each such individual and universe logically leads us to admit that it (one similar to it) had existed at least once before, in some form or the other. This amounts to saying that the series of births an individual had already completed or the series of creation the (human) universe (universes) has (have) been through has no beginning. Both God and human individuals (considered as a self) are eternal but the human individuals as an embodied soul is created and has a beginning and as such any single life of such an individual is one in a beginningless series of births and deaths interspersed with individual deaths or periods of dissolution of the created universe. It is a very technical thesis and takes a lot of effort to understand. It means that the created time or periods of time has no beginning. But the contradiction will vanish if we understand it to mean that the series of the successive periods of (created) time has no beginning and in that sense is even eternal, but within it the created periods are not eternal but have beginnings. We do not like to pursue the matter any more here but simply note that the multiple life view of human individual has many consequences that are not easily intelligible to the single life view of human individual shared in common by both Christianity and the modern European civilization.

To come back to cosmology and arrow of time, according to the modern cosmologists the arrow or arrows of time point towards greater and greater disorder. Hence scientifically speaking the world is heading towards greatest disorder, which is the scientific analogue of dissolution. This is contrary to the view of progress in any culture. Even the cultures where dissolution is to be met after an incredibly long time progress, especially in the social and worldly spheres, is marked by increasingly greater order as is enshrined in various institutions of family and social life. To take greater and greater organization, more and more organized bodies, material, biological, or social as more and more disordered states is simply to revolt against the established usages and beliefs supported not only by commonsense, which may not be scientifically very sophisticated, but even according to the evolutionary view. The cosmologist's explanation is that even when we find increase of order within smaller and closed systems like an individual's active brain, or organizations like family or state, or even this universe, outside these systems there would be as much or more disorder. Thus, in the universe as a whole there will always be increase in disorder. All these follow if we accept the second law of thermodynamics. But the question is, does this law have its exemplification or application outside the mathematical model, to the functioning of the human mind or life of man and social progress?[83] In other words does the cosmological arrow of time obeying the law of entropy increase in the realm of social

83. It may seem that it has application in the field of human "mind" in view of the fact that now the concept of entropy is used in information theory. Actually, however, in the thesis that the gain in entropy means loss of information the word information is used not only in a quantitative sense but also in a highly technical sense. On the other hand, when Schrodinger speaks of the importance of negative entropy in biology he shows that any living organism delays its death, that is, its decay into thermal equilibrium. It does so by its ability to maintain itself in a fairly high level of orderliness, i.e. fairly low level of entropy by continually absorbing negative entropy from its environment. See G.J. Whitrow's article in Paul Edward (ed.), *Encyclopedia of Philosophy*, vol. 2 (Macmilan Publishing, 1967), p. 528.

progress, does it point at the same direction as the arrow of progress? As is expected an affirmative answer has been returned. But when put in common words and illustrated with ordinary examples the explanation seems to be too forced and sophistical.[84] The main assumption is that matter is an ordered state compared to energy, which is a state of disorder. The beginning of the universe is the expansion following the exploding of the matter at the big-bang. While the universe is expanding it is also creating matter — elementary particles to galaxies and stars. All these are ordered states created in course of transformation of the infinitely dense matter into energy. But it is quite possible to prove that in the very process of formation or creation of order the energy spent increases the total amount of energy in the universe. The next step is too simple or too neat to carry conviction. Energy is a state of disorder compared to matter, which indicates a state of order. Any organized state leads to the increment of disorder somewhere. We are not becoming more and more organized in our personal, social or spiritual life. Or this does not indicate that we are progressing. Progress of time is inversely related to the progress of man.

One may think that there is a saving fact. When we speak of our earth we are speaking of one single locality of a very huge and growing system called the universe. In the overall picture of the universe, which is much larger than our world, taking the word literally, entropy increase is a law but this does not mean that there cannot be local fluctuations. It is most certain that ultimately the disorderliness would be infinite and all matter would be converted into energy but that is too far a future to affect the established habits of beliefs of man, his speech and action. One at this stage can hardly

84. Hawking, pp. 160-61.

help saying, though the remark may be regarded as simplistic and amateurish, which to some extent it is, that the scientific cosmology is so far removed from our empirical life and culture that it seems to be more a speculative theory than an empirical science. And though on many other counts it has some advantage the philosophical theory considered above has a good chance of being accepted as a good scientific explanation if not a science. So far we do not find any way of combining advanced and scientifically good philosophical explanation, that match most of our established world-view — beliefs, practices, values and so on — with the current cosmological view which is otherwise a grand speculative theory. What can be more theoretically and culturally rewarding than if they could be combined?

2

Time and its Knowledge[1]

Sukha Ranjan Saha

SCIENTISTS and philosophers are equally and greatly interested in the concept of time. It is mostly held that time is eternal and infinite in nature, though a small minority holds a different view in the matter. It is not my interest to probe into such issues. The familiar division of time into past, present and future seems more interesting to many including the masters of Nyāya philosophy, namely, Gautama and Vātsyāyana. They examine a position that seeks to do away with the concept of the present and defend it in a novel manner. We propose to discuss their views in some detail. The question, how do we know time, is also a very interesting problem. We have tried to present the Advaita Vedānta position that time is known in what they call *sākṣī-jñāna* and have tried to argue that it comes closer to the Kantian position of a priori intuition.

Time is one of the most important concepts in philosophy inasmuch as every system has something or the other to say about it. Look at the Upaniṣadic statement, *sadeva souma idamagra āsīt*[2] in which it is claimed "everything was existent

---

1. A different version of the paper is published in Sukharanjan Saha, *Epistemology in Prachina and Navya Nyāya* (Kolkata: Jadavpur University, 2003).

2. *Chāndogyopaniṣad* 6.2.

before." In the Kāla-Sūkta of the *Atharvaveda*,[3] time has been claimed to be something from which everything arose. Again, we are all familiar with the fourfold division into *Satya*, *Tretā*, *Dvāpara* and *Kali yuga*s and we are afraid that because of the heavier scale of *adharma*s we may have to face fatal consequences when the lord appears in the form of an *avatāra* to restore the balance in favour of *dharma* by destroying the world of *adharma*, as has been said in the *Gīta*.

I

According to Buddhism everything is momentary and we presume that time also falls within the scope of this theory. If so time is momentary. There is an oddity involved in this stand at least as far as Buddhism is concerned. It is held in this system that not only nothing lasts beyond a moment but also that no two such things share any property in common — for had that not been the case their commitment to absolute pluralism would have been groundless. They express this by saying that everything is *svalakṣaṇa* and also that everything that a thing has is unique. But apparently, at least, there will be some difficulty as everything that is (exists) belongs to a given moment of time. Thus, being in time seems to be something that belongs to everything. Therefore, this feature of being in time is a shareable feature and not really anything exclusive or unique. The Buddhists will not accept the cogency of the argument, and the claim that being in time is a shareable feature is dismissed as mere sophistry. As nobody can bathe twice in the same river, so also no two things belong to any given specific moment of time. What people take to be one single continuous time is nothing but an illusion and therefore the claim that being in time is a shareable feature is equally

3. Kālasūkta, *Atharvaveda*, 19.53-54

illusory. What we take to be running time is nothing but a series of successive moments no two of which are identical. As the whole is not anything different from the parts, so also a series is tentatively nothing different from its members. Thus, time is nothing more than the discrete moments.

There is a section of Jaina philosophers who admit that time has slices which are likened to atoms and the view is referred to as *kālaparamāṇuvāda*. The analogy of atomic units may have its inherent difficulties. But one point seems to be worth noting here. Though time is conceivable as extending *ad infinitum* in both the directions of the past and the future and thus is to be regarded as infinite in some sense, this theory under reference denies this viewpoint. For, according to this theory, the seemingly continuous time is at best a composite thing comprising the atoms or slices of time. And nothing composite can be infinite as its limits are, theoretically speaking, identifiable. The lesson that we may derive from the Buddhist theory as well as from the Jaina view under reference is that however strong an inclination we may feel for the view that time is one and infinite, this can be consistently countered by the Buddhist or the Jaina theory that time as an entity is not anything infinite. This tension is sometimes sought to be resolved by some philosophers, particularly the Vaiśeṣikas and the later Naiyāyikas, by a hypothesis that time is both an infinite eternal single thing and also has slices which though not identifiable with the single infinite TIME, may be identified with non-eternal things of limited magnitude that are in time.

The words these philosophers use for referring to these two types of time are *mahākāla* and *khaṇḍakāla*. If we understand the component *mahā* as standing for infinite magnitude the expression *mahākāla* will signify infinite time. The other expression *khaṇḍakāla* which contains the component *khaṇḍa*, meaning "part" will not stand for infinite time. But in reality this infinite time which is supposed to be the necessary condition for any effect to take place cannot have parts, as it is not a composite entity consisting of parts like created substances. Keeping this in mind philosophers sometimes refer to time as *jagadādhāra*, literally meaning the substratum of the world or *jagat*. The word *jagat* here is understood as the totality of all effects.

Philosophers in the Nyāya-Vaiśeṣika tradition uphold the view that in order for something to be perceptible the thing must have colour in it. The stipulation excludes all substances other than earth, water and fire substances as non-perceptible. Those who want to include air from the list of perceptible substances state that a perceptible substance must have either colour or touch in it. Time is held to be a substance as it has at least the qualities of number and magnitude in it; but as it does not have either colour or touch it cannot thus be regarded as a perceptible substance.

Now, if time is not a perceptible substance how can we come to the view that it is existent and is of such and such nature. Philosophers of the Vaiśeṣika and later Nyāya schools resort to some sophisticated type of inference as proof for the existence of time and in this they utilize the noted fact of time's being the substratum of any effectuation whatsoever. They also sometimes refer to an additional fact that we often take something as younger/older in relation to something else. It is held that this may also serve as the basis for inferring the existence of running time without reference to which a given thing cannot be so held to be younger or older. But other philosophers reject this plea on general grounds. They argue that inference is not possible without invariable concomitance which must be noticed as obtaining between concerned terms. But *ex hypothesis* since time is not perceptible this relationship cannot be claimed to be capable of being established. Hence the proposed inference is not possible.

In the Vaiśeṣika tradition Vallabha in his *Nyāyalīlāvatī*[4] and his commentators in their commentaries thereon, and in the Advaita tradition Citsukha in his *Tattvapradīpikā*[5] and his commentators in their commentaries thereon continued this debate for a long period. Relevant issues were taken up by later thinkers in both the traditions in their independent works without there being in sight any resolution of the debate till now. But what we miss in this debate is the examination of concepts of the past, present and future associated with the concept of time. Happily for us, however, we find a discussion on time from such a perspective in Gautama's *Nyāyasūtras* and Vātsyāyana's commentary on them. Philosophers of the later period did not find the issue interesting enough to address themselves to it. But in our opinion we should acquaint ourselves with the views of Gautama and Vātsyāyana.

II

Gautama's *Sūtras*[6] on time are placed just after his *Sūtras* on detailed examination of *anumāna pramāṇa*. According to Gautama there are three types of *anumāna* or inferences in two of which we proceed either from the perception of the effect to the existence of the antecedent as by seeing the swelling of the river one infers that there had been a rainfall or in the reverse way, from the perception of gathering of clouds in the sky one infers that there will soon be rain. In both the cases the relationship between the terms of causal

---

4. Vallabha's *Nyāyalīlāvatī* (Benares: Chowkhamba, 1934) pp. 279-93.
5. *Citsukha's Tattvapradīpikā*, 2nd edn. (Varanasi: Saddarshan Prakashan, 1974) pp. 510-20.
6. *Nyāyasūtras* 2.1.39-43

chain, knowledge of which is at the basis of inference, is temporal in nature. Again Vātsyāyana characterizes inference as a source of knowledge which can give us knowledge of things of the past, present or future while perception is restricted only to the realm of the present. It is therefore natural for them to undertake an examination of the concepts of the past, present and future in the context of inference. An objection has first been raised to the effect that the concept of the present is not essential for the other two concepts and therefore it is not necessary to admit the existence of the present in addition to the two others. The objection is then set aside by them.

The objector begins with the example of a falling body. It is usually believed that the activity of falling may be understood at an intermediate stage to have the following features: (1) it has fallen in the preceding time from a certain place up to a certain distance, (2) it is falling now at the present time, and (3) and since it has not yet reached the bottom it will fall further down in succeeding time. But this hypothesis is rejected by the objector. He wants to establish his point by referring to the path of a falling body. Let us spatially represent the path by a line. We can then identify a given point in the line and say the falling body has already traversed it. This length may be taken to correspond to what is called the past. But think of the other stretch of the line which the falling body is still to traverse. Since this has not already been traversed in the past this will have to be traversed in the future. Therefore, the time the falling body will require to traverse is divided into two parts, namely, the past and the future. It thus leaves no room for the present.

Gautama and Vātsyāyana reject the contention of the objector by pointing out the fact that time cannot be understood by spatial analogy. A spatial line can be conceived to be divisible into two parts without leaving any remainder. But this picture cannot be true of time, for it is not justifiable to hold that time consists only of the past and the future without the present intervening between the two. Vātsyāyana points out that the distinctive character of time can be understood best by reference to activity. And using the same example of a falling body he says that the present is when the activity is on, that is, when the body is falling, the past being the time taken by this body in falling that is over and the future being the time to be taken by it for falling further.

The objector may like to continue with his stand and would argue that we are familiar with pairs of words like "large and small," "shade and light," etc. in which the referent of the one is just the opposite of the other. The words themselves are taken as relative words the meanings of which are to be understood with reference to one another. Such is the case with reference to the pair of words "past and future." Therefore, while talking about time we need not go beyond the past and the future and the hypothesis of the present can be dispensed with. Vātsyāyana says in reply that there are other familiar pairs of words such as "colour and touch"/ "taste and small" in which meanings are not identified with reference to one another. Thus, if we want to determine the meanings of the words "past" and "future" in this way we must be able to offer additional justification. Moreover, even when a pair of words are held to be relative, their meanings cannot all be determined by mutual reference. For in that case there will be palpable circularity. In the case under consideration if the present is not admitted the past will have to be understood as what is not the future and the future as what is not the past. But in such a case not only the two concepts are to be defined with reference to one another but in the understanding of the one an idea of the other is presupposed.

We shall thus move in a vicious circle. In elucidation of his positive stand Vātsyāyana proceeds to explain how we may be said to be able to grasp the present.

Consistently with his stand that time cannot be understood properly in the analogy of a spatial path but only by reference to activity Vātsyāyana goes on to offer an explication of the concept of activity. He, thus, refers to the distinction in language between names and verbs. Finite verbs, that is, verbs used in agreement with nominatives and indicating case, mood and tense are broadly categorised as action-words or *kriyā-pada*s, though all such verbs do not always represent any activity. Thus, the verb *bhū* and *as* meaning "to exist"/ "to become" do not represent any activity on the part of the referent of the nominative word. For example, when we say *ghaṭo asti* "the pot exists" we do not speak of any activity on the part of the pot. Strictly speaking, the verbs with agreeing nominatives which stand for conscious agents are mostly indicative of activity. Such an activity implies change in bodily condition. Thus, when we say, "he is going" we mean that the person is moving from one place to another perhaps on foot. Or, when we say that "he is cooking" we mean to say that the person is preparing food through a process which involves not only movement of his limbs but also handling of the materials for food and other necessary accessories according to a plan and design. Since physical movement is involved in such activities we speak of action also in cases where activity is not involved as in such cases where conscious desire and planning are absent, say, when one makes the observation "the apple is falling." We may contrast such statements as just noted from other statements which agree with these statements in all respects except the tenses that are involved. On the semantic plane time corresponds to the tenses. If we are justified in allowing this correlation between the syntactical differences in the statements and their semantic counterparts, then as even the objector admits the existence of the past and of the future, the third type of semantic counterpart corresponding to the features present in the statements quoted will certainly be different from the past and the future and is thus designated as the present. Vātsyāyana points out that the verbs used in the other tenses in similar types of statements refer to actions which have already been completed or are still to be completed, thus indicating the existence of the past and the future.

When our experience is about pleasurable things and we want to enjoy it for longer period the specious present eludes our grasp and promptly recedes into the past. But this is not always the case, for when something is not so, its experience seems to be monotonously continuing, or at least we feel that way. But perhaps this was not in his mind when Vātsyāyana stated that the present may not be always that elusive. He gives us the example of the activity of cooking which consists of a series of smaller bits of work envisaged in planning the act of cooking. When we refer to the complete series and not to the smaller bits by other appropriate words, the entire stretch of time represented by the words "is cooking" represents to us a longer stretch of time than the one represented by, say, "is washing the vegetables." Our experience of the present, Vātsyāyana further points out, is not restricted to its representation by the relevant uses of the action verbs. Even where a verb is not indicative of actions but does have similar syntactical features as in *ghaṭo asti* and *poṭo asti* it indicates the present time.

Gautama and Vātsyāyana conclude their defence of the concept of the present by an epistemological argument. According to them knowledge is of different varieties. Non-perceptual knowledge is basically distinct from perception.

But it is nevertheless dependent on perception in some way or the other. Perception is necessarily such that it is about that which exists. If something is not-existent, that is, if it is a thing of the past or of the future or absolutely non-existent like the hare's horn or barren mother there cannot be any perception of it. Though, theoretically speaking, the past thing could be and was perhaps an object of past perception or the future thing may be an object of future perception, the fictitious type of non-existent object can never be an object of perception. In fact, perception testifies to the existence of its object at the time of perception. Thus, there is a correlation between the time of perception and the time of existence of its object. We are constantly in possession of perception of this or that object. Therefore, if we look at the goings on of mind and identify an act of perception at any given moment then its object will be coexistent with the act at the time. If we are not greatly bothered with the starry vision when stars may not be existing or with the illusory appearance we can say that for the percipient his act of perception is not a thing of the past or of the future and therefore for him it defines the present. Hence this cognitive act and its object, if it is not to be rejected for any reason, are the best examples of the present. If we are not unduly sceptical and accept the possibility of knowledge and of perception, the present is very much real. It has in it the stamp of difference from the past and also the future. Hence, what we understand by time is real in all its facets.

III

But how do we know time? I would like to say that we know time in the most direct way as we know ourselves. I further believe that such a thesis was not unacceptable to the past masters we were talking about. It is true that they have defined perception by reference to sensory contact. On a restricted interpretation this may be construed as missing in respect of time. But the later Naiyāyikas interpreted God's omnipotence as a kind of direct knowledge though it is not due to sensory contact. The Prabhākara philosophers define perception as *sākṣāt-jñāna* and the Advaitins accept a kind of direct awareness called *sākṣī-jñāna* which also has no sensory origin. We can also utilize these theories in answering the question how we come to know time. And we should not also forget that the great Immanuel Kant of the other tradition admitted a priori (non-sensory) intuition of space and time.[7]

The thesis that perception is due to sensory contact with the object presupposes:

1. Perception is an effect and not contemporaneous with its object even when it is itself an effect.
2. A given sense organ is necessary for a given type of perception.
3. The object must exist previously so that the sense organ can be in contact with it for giving rise to the perception.

These presuppositions have been challenged by many philosophers. Thus, many philosophers deny that the object of perception must exist antecedently to the act of perception. They argue that there are things which do not remain unnoticed at any stage of their duration. Thus, the self is constantly revealed to the knower. Hence, there is no possibility of its coming into contact with a sense organ during an unnoticed phase. What has been said of the self is also true of the states of the self such as cognition, pleasure, pain, desire, aversion and determination. It is true that these are not durable like their substratum. But even then, like the self, these also do not have any unnoticed phase of existence. Hence, the

7. Immanuel Kant, *The Critique of Pure Reason, Transcendental Aesthetic*, tr. N.K. Smith (London: Macmillan, 1929).

question whether sensory contact is necessary for their awareness is a pointless one. Therefore, in such cases, the direct awareness about objects which is also called *pratyakṣa* in our tradition cannot be due to the operation of the sense organ. Thus, *pratyakṣa* theory of *Tripuṭīsaṁvit* envisages that in the awareness of the self and its cognition, no sensory contact is necessary. The Advaitin endorses this theory and holds that such a variety of awareness, which is direct in nature and is yet not due to sensory contact of any kind is what is called *asākṣī-jñāna*. The awareness about the mental states of pleasure, pain and similar others is of the same kind.

The Naiyāyikas do not accept that the self or its properties under reference necessarily get noticed and that these can have a new phase of existence. Therefore, our direct awareness should also be due to the operation of some sense organ. They are conscious that none of the five external sense organs called the *manas* account for the origin of the kind of direct awareness under discussion. But others deny the cogency of this thesis of the unnoticed phase of existence of the self and its properties and also of the postulation of the sixth sense organ. And even if we spare the Naiyāyika here what will he do in respect of our awareness of time? As they themselves say: time is the cause of every effect; it will have to be there before that awareness takes place. But how can we say that it is there without some kind of epistemic backing? Hence, like the accessible properties of the self, Time also cannot have any unnoticed phase of existence. And if so, the way these other things get noticed in the Prabhākara system, *sākṣi-pratyakṣa* in Advaita Vedānta or a priori sensible intuition as in Kant for none of which sense organ has any role to play, time also gets noticed by us.

3

Time as Power
A Brief Survey of Bhartṛhari's Metaphysics

Tandra Patnaik

A DEEP look at the philosophical tradition of India reveals that in most of the systems, time or *kāla* is regarded as an important element of the phenomenal or empirical world. But unlike in the West, here, a subtle distinction is maintained between the notion of causality and time. When the Indian metaphysicians talk of causality they do not understand it as a matter of the antecedent and the consequent determined in terms of time, for according to the Indian tradition time is not linear in nature, but cyclic. The Indian philosophical systems bring in the notion of causality, mostly, in the context of the creation of the universe. Besides, these philosophers understand causality in terms of material cause and efficient cause. Therefore, the concept of time is discussed generally in the context of the relation between the ultimate Reality and the empirical world. While talking of the empirical world they unanimously accept that the world is characterized by change and continuity. So, depending on their respective metaphysical position, time is conceived either as a real substance or a mental construct: a series of atoms or else an undivided whole. Surprisingly enough, the concept of time has not been offered the prominence it deserves in most of the systems (excepting in certain schools of Buddhism and in Jainism). So it appears perplexing that the grammarian philosopher Bhartṛhari deviates from the tradition to conceive time as the primary link between the Reality and the empirical world. In his *magnum opus*, a three-part treatise, entitled *Vākyapadīya* he makes not only frequent reference to this but devotes an entire section to the concept of time, entitled *Kālasamuddeśa*. Here, I will attempt to explore the possible reasons for Bhartṛhari's dependence on this concept while other classical systems ignore it.

Bhartṛhari (fifth century) is affiliated more to the school of grammar than philosophy. He is supposed to carry on the great tradition of the *vaiyākaraṇika*s starting with the great Pāṇini to Patañjali and Kātyāyana. But Bhartṛhari ventured to think of himself as a *śabda-pramāṇaka* (the philosopher of language) too.[1] That is why his treatise *Vākyapadīya* deals more with a form of linguistic monism rather than the foundational principles of grammar. An unbiased look at the history of Indian metaphysics reveals that he was one of the earliest propounders of Advaitism (non-dualism). For him, the ultimate reality is *śabda-tattva*, i.e. the speech-principle, the logos as the absolute and creative principles. In the opening line of his treatise he declares:

> The highest Reality (*Brahman*) is of the nature of *śabda*. It is without beginning and end. Thus it is the highest principle. This eternal and immutable principle manifests itself as the objects and processes (*jagat prakriyā*) of the universe.
>
> — *Vākyapadīya* 1.1

This metaphysical position may appear very perplexing. But in some sense it is an extension of the Vedic line of thought.[2]

1. Bhartṛhari, *Mahābhāṣya Dīpikā*, part I (Poona: Bhandarkar Oriental series, 1967), pp. 16-18.
2. *Taittirīya Brāhmaṇa*, II.2.4.2.

In his commentary on this above-mentioned aphorism, Bhartṛhari clarifies that:

> All worldly manifestations, though appearing to be distinct from one another, are of the nature of words because in all of them the *śabda*/word-principle persists, because we know the world through words and all our cognition is intertwined with words. All objects through their beginning, sustenance and end can be determined only through words. — *Vākyapadīya* 1.1

There is nothing very mystical about this sort of explanation. The world that exists is a matter of our knowledge and experience. All sorts of knowledge including our awareness of facts are possible because we assign a name (*nāma*) and form (*rūpa*) to them. We think, conceptualize and become conscious of everything through our potential to associate them with words. In this context one may very validly ask — why does Bhartṛhari define *Brahman* in terms of *śabda-tattva* rather than defining it in terms of *sat, cit, ānanda* (as it has been done in the Upaniṣads and the Advaita philosophy)? Bhartṛhari, clearing his metaphysical position, states that as a *śabda-pramāṇaka* or the philosopher of language his primary concern is not with what the world actually is, but how it is cognized, conceptualized and represented through words. Thus, the notion of *śabda-Brahman* logically follows from his metaphysical position.

In his metaphysical scheme the *śabda-Brahman* is conceived as one and eternal but manifesting itself as diverse and changeable in the form of the phenomenal world. Therefore, like any other monist he faces the problem of explaining the relation between the Absolute Reality and the empirical world guided by relativity. The Advaitin Śaṅkara takes resort to the concepts *māyā* and *avidyā* to explain the relation between the Reality and the world. Bhartṛhari, on the other hand, introduces the concept of *kāla* and *avidyā* in keeping with his position as a linguistic monist. Here lies the novelty of his approach *vis-à-vis* Śaṅkara. For Śaṅkara, *māyā* is the principle of projection and *avidyā* is the principle of concealment. But Bhartṛhari's use of *kāla* and *avidyā* have different implications. Helārāja, the famous commentator on the third canto of *Vākyapadīya*, very clearly indicates that "the power called *avidyā* is responsible for the One becoming many, i.e. for the emergence of the phenomenal world. The power called Time (*kāla*) is responsible for the phenomena appearing in temporal sequence."[3] In fact, the very conception of temporal sequence holds the clue to Bhartṛhari's conception of the phenomenal world. The notions of continuity and change that characterizes the empirical world can only be understood in terms of temporal sequence. The world consists of an infinite number of changing objects. Change means states and processes through which objects pass. According to Bhartṛhari all objects pass through at least three states, i.e. origin, continuity and destruction.[4] This presupposes temporal sequence. Again change presupposes objects that undergo change. On the other hand, they are the products of previous processes and actions. Thus, the empirical world can be better understood in terms of temporal sequence. Somehow, most of the classical systems of Indian philosophy seem to miss this point. It appears that Bhartṛhari's metaphysical approach puts him in an advantageous position. Unless the notion of time is brought in as one of the key concepts in explaining the relation between the Reality as the eternal and unchangeable principle, and the empirical world as characterized by change, the gap between the two seems unbridgeable.

---

3. Bhartṛhari, *Vākyapadīya* (vol. I), ed. & tr. K.A.S. Iyer (Pune: Deccan College, 1969) (Section 1.6-7) p. 201.
4. *Vākyapadīya,* III.3.

His conception of *Brahman* as *śabda* has deep connection with his theory of *kāla*. According to him, the linguistic principle in its highest stage is unified and one, but it is manifested in diverse concepts and linguistic forms to find final expression in the form of uttered words. Our utterances are sequential. We cannot express all that we think or cognize simultaneously. It has to be expressed syllable by syllable. By the time one syllable is uttered it is replaced by another. Thus, the non-sequential, unified speech potency is transformed into a sequential and diversified form. Based on this, Bhartṛhari formulates a metaphysical position wherein the world can be represented as a series of sequences. In other words, the world is not a totality of things/objects but a totality of events or states of affair. The events cannot be explained without reference to time. This may be the primary reason why Bhartṛhari conceives *kāla* as a power (*śakti*). Before we examine how successfully he explains the relation between the notion of *kālaśakti* and the sequential nature of the phenomenal world, I would prefer to discuss in brief his theory of *kāla*.

I have stated earlier that according to Bhartṛhari the one and unified *śabda-Brahman* manifests itself in diversified names and forms. This is beyond the comprehension of the ordinary cognizers (being under the spell of *avidyā*). This is responsible for the presentation of the One as diverse. He justifies his position with the help of the following simile:

> Just as in the yolk of the peacock's egg diverse colours of the plumes are present in an undifferentiated stage, similarly within the *śabda-tattva* endless varieties of colour, taste, form and sound are dormant in an undifferentiated state.
>
> — *Vākyapadīya*, I.51

This undifferentiated state is manifested due to the power of *Brahman*, which is known as *kālaśakti*. The very first canto of *Vākyapadīya*, which largely deals with this metaphysical position, provides the crucial clue to his analysis of the concept of time. In a sense it provides the gist of what he discusses elaborately in *Kālasamuddeśa*. It is stated, "depending on whose (*Brahman*'s) Time-power (though one) differentiation, the six — birth, transformation, etc. — become the cause of all variety in Being."[5] In his commentary on his own aphorism Bhartṛhari elaborates:

> All powers depending on their causes and having a starting point are governed by the creative power (*svatantrya*) called time: they follow the modes of this Time-power. Because of the regulation of the immense diversity of each object by means of prevention and permission, its appearances seem to have a sequence. Time, by allowing them to come to be, is the secondary cause of all transformations, which depend on their own other causes also and whose production has been delayed. Its causal power being thus differentiated by manifestations, which have a sequence, the differentiated, which exists in the manifestation, is attributed to it. It is like attributing to the balance the divisions marked by lines on it at the time of balancing of weight of the material, which is in contact with it.[6]

Thus, when sequence is attributed to something which is neither prior nor posterior in the form "it was" or "it was not," the six — birth, transformation, etc. — become the source of modifications, the changes in Being. We can be in a better position to understand Bhartṛhari's position if we examine the implications of the above remarks in detail.

1. Time is the most important power of the *Brahman*. It is therefore called *svātantrya śakti*, i.e. the creative power. Helārāja in his commentary on the work[7] interprets

5. *Vākyapadīya*, I.3
6. Ibid.
7. Ibid., III.9.12.

svatantrya śakti as the "power of complete freedom of *Brahman*." It is also the all-pervading (*vibhu*). It is the very soul of the universe.[8] According to K.A.S. Iyer, the famous scholar on Bhartṛhari, there is no difference between the *Brahman* and his power called Time because Bhartṛhari himself states about his own remark "(*Brahman*) though not different from his powers, seems to be so."[9] In this sense there is no difference between the wielder of power and the power itself. Again, time understood in the sense of a creative power is compared to the stage manager (*sūtradhāra*) of the puppet show, which pulls the strings and makes the puppets dance.[10] It is due to time that the unmanifested potentialities are realised. So Bhartṛhari calls it the *kāla* because it brings forth (*kālayati*) objects out of their causes. Just as a mechanic turns the water wheel, similarly, the Almighty turns all phenomena through its power called *kāla*. So it is known as *kālaśakti*, the Time-Power.

2. Bhartṛhari maintains a distinction between time as a causal power and its manifestation as a sequence. *Kālaśakti* is one and eternal. But it appears as differentiated in moments, hours, past, present and the future. Time is one and all-pervasive from the transcendental standpoint, but from an empirical standpoint it appears to be divided into sequences. The attribution of sequence to the sequenceless and eternal *kālaśakti* is due to our attribution of sequence to it. Time itself is not sequential.

---

8. *Vākyapadīya*, III.9.12.
9. Ibid., I.2.
10. Ibid., III.9.4.

> As objects are constantly changing, something is always being produced and something else is always perishing. This sequence which belongs to objects is attributed to Time. Sequence is primarily the property of actions but it is attributed to something else.
>
> — *Vākyapadīya*, III, 9.30, Helārāja's Commentary

There is neither prior nor posterior in time as such. It is due to our association of Time with activity and sequences that we talk of time as prior or posterior.

3. *Kālaśakti* symbolizes the manifestations of the world in an evolution, which involves actions and processes. All animate and inanimate things are liable to change. This is classified into six states such as birth, existence, alteration, growth, decay, and destruction. Thus, the empirical world is analysed more in terms of actions and processes than objects. This may be inferred from Bhartṛhari's emphasis on the notion of the sequential nature of the world. The notion of time cannot be understood without conceiving the world as constituted of actions and processes, i.e., *kriyā-vivartta*. If the question of process is not there, there is no necessity of bringing in time as the key concept in the explanation of the nature of the empirical world. He categorically states "Time is the very soul of the universe. Hence it is identified with activity itself."[11] Helārāja in his commentary on the above aphorism says "in the well regulated stages of birth, sustenance, and destruction the activity of Time is inevitable. So it runs like a thread right through everything in the universe. Being the cause of all activity, it is sometimes identified with time itself." Thus action and process

11. *Vākyapadīya*, III.9.12.

are the key concepts in Bhartṛhari's analysis of the relation between the Time and the world.

4. Time-power controls the cosmic activities, which are immensely diverse. The diversity needs to be controlled through a certain order. This order comes from the two powers of the time, i.e. permission (*abhyānujñā*) and prevention (*pratibandha*). He says, "the regulation of birth or manifestation depends upon the operation of powers. The sustenance of objects is also regulated through it." Not only should there be the beginning of states and activities but they must also continue. The function of permission therefore is to regulate the birth and continuity of an object. Any object that has beginning continues to exist because it is capable of fulfilling some purpose with the help of other co-operating objects. As it fulfils various purposes it is conceived to have continuity. When the objects are no longer able to fulfil their purposes, this is also due to time. This function is known as prevention (*pratibandha*). By it, the capacities of the objects are obstructed.[12] Bhartṛhari says, if time did not prevent or did not remove prevention, the states (of a being) would be confused, deprived of priority and posteriority. In the absence of such functions there would be no law of sequence, and without sequence such confusions as seeds, sprouts, stalk and stem would take place. Therefore, the sequence maintained through prevention and permission is absolutely necessary.[13]

5. Since the process of the world is sequential it has to be understood in terms of past, present and future. So

---

12. *Vākyapadīya*, III.9.23-24.

13. Ibid., III.9.4-5.

Bhartṛhari accepts the empirical reality of these three states. In fact, he calls them the functions of time along with prevention, permission, sequence and decay. He states that "conditioned by action, Time attains the states of past, future and present."[14] Commenting on this Helārāja elaborates, "Time, conditioned by an action which, after having been initiated, is over, is called the past. When conditioned by actions, whose accessories are present and which are accepted to be initiated soon, it is called the future. When conditioned by actions, which have been initiated but not finished, it is called the present." The past is that where the action is over but it is preserved in the memory. The forms of objects, which are expected to come and are reflected in the mind, are called the future. That past objects can be preserved in memory and future objects can be conceived as objects yet to come can be expressed in words. This proves that past and future are as real as the present itself. This is possible because of the two primary powers of time. The past and the future are matters of prevention and the present is a matter of permission. The three time divisions — past, present and future — are three courses like roads. Just as travellers continuously come and go on roads, similarly beings experiencing transformation in these three courses perform a continuous series of appearance and disappearance.[15]

In this context it is worthwhile to discuss the position of the Mādhyamika School of Buddhism as presented by Bhartṛhari himself. (He follows the unique style incorporating

14. *Vākyapadīya*, III.9.37.

15. Ibid., III.9.74.

the prevalent views on the topic under discussion in his work, not necessarily as *pratipakṣa*. As a result, sometimes it becomes difficult to discern which is his view and which that of others.) According to them the "present" does not have an independent status as a part of the sequence. They argue that if an action is a process, a series of moments, then the moment that is past is something which has been accomplished. As far as that moment is concerned, action is past. As far as the moment that is coming is concerned, action is still in the future. There cannot be a moment, which is both past and future, existent and non-existent at the same time. Therefore, action cannot be anything else than past or future. There cannot be a middle state in between. Besides, many moments cannot coexist together. Only one moment (present) can be perceived at a time. And in that moment there is no sequence. What is called present cannot be the same as the fact of being a sequence or a process because we cannot perceive such a sequence in a moment. Therefore, there is no such thing as action consisting of sequence. We never perceive the sequence. Hence, we cannot remember it. Nor can we look upon many moments as one action because some of the moments are past and some are yet to come, i.e. some are existent and others non-existent. How can the action be said to be composed of contradictory elements? So, according to the Mādhyamikas there are distinct moments, which have one common feature — action. The common feature can only be the fact or fitness of being produced. Thus, action is a common feature existing in each moment and it cannot be a sequence of moments.[16] Refuting this viewpoint, Bhartṛhari states, action is one, it is a sequence of moments having one purpose. It is one because it has one purpose. Even though some moments are existent and others

16. *Vākyapadīya*, III.85-87.

are not there can be a present moment. The present should be defined as "the fact of having been begun but not yet finished." A sequence of moments, all leading to the same result, if looked upon as one even before the result is produced can be said to be present. It is this unity which can produce the result. So every moment in the sequence can be said to be the present. Again the whole thing can be looked upon from another angle. When a series of momentary acts are cognized within and are reflected in one act of cognition, that is said to be its oneness and its presentness.[17] There can be a mental unification of things, which can be experienced in succession, because the impressions of what was experienced are still fresh. It is only in this way that one can explain the cognition of collections. What has been experienced as succession can, however, be remembered simultaneously.[18]

I have stated earlier that excepting some schools of Buddhism and in Jainism, most of the classical schools of Indian philosophy accept that the world is a totality of objects, either real or phenomenal. Though Buddhism believes in momentariness of the world process, it emphasizes "series" rather than "sequence." This may be one of the reasons why time is not regarded as the primary bond between the moments.

Finally, I come to another important concept, which has been considered along with *kālaśakti* to be responsible for the appearance of One as many, i.e. the concept of *avidyā*. According to Helārāja, Bhartṛhari speaks quite clearly about the distinct functions of *avidyā* and *kālaśakti*. The former is responsible for bringing out differentiation in the undifferentiated *Brahman* and the latter is responsible for the

17. *Vākyapadīya*, III.9.90.

18. Helārāja's commentary on *Vākyapadīya*, III.9.90.

temporal sequence in which the differentiated phenomena are presented to the individual perceiver.[19] *Avidyā* is responsible for the limitations in our cognition. So our cognition can never grasp the whole object. Object is a kind of mental construct (*vikalpa*) which involves selection and elimination. The pure object can neither be cognized or expressed in words. As Bhartṛhari indicates, "nothing is one or many, nothing is white or not-white itself. It is due to association with others things that substances appear this way or that way."[20] So, according to Helārāja, Bhartṛhari believes that the phenomenal world consists of objects (*mūrti-vivartta*) and their actions (*kriyā-vivartta*), but objects as such are only conceivable in terms of states and processes; and they have to be sequentially placed. Therefore Bhartṛhari's metaphysical structure would have collapsed had he not offered central a position to *kāla* or time.

---

19. *Vākyapadīya*, III.1.15-16.
20. Ibid., III.9.7.

4

A Perspective on Time in Language and Grammar

Ganesh Prasad Panda

STUDIES on time have attracted the attention of scholars belonging to different disciplines since long. It is a vital issue for many disciplines and hence a matter for interdisciplinary research. Since it is a multidimensional concept, elaborate attempts are made to elucidate its very nature and yet it remains a matter of controversy. Approaches to and methods applied to time vary from period to period and from person to person. While nothing final can be said about time certain fundamental attempts were made by ancient Indian thinkers which are noteworthy.*

There are, as mentioned earlier, various approaches to the definition and use of time. Yet time remains an inevitable presence encompassing all spheres of human activity. It is here that language comes into the picture. Being a vital instrument of human expression and communication, it is not independent of time. But it remains to be seen what aspect of language brings itself in touch with time. There can be several levels at which time influences language. In this chapter I shall discuss a few of them.

---

* See Schayer, Stainslaw, "Contribution to the Prohlem of Time in Indian Philosophy," *Essays on Time in Buddhism*, ed. H.S. Prasad (Delhi: Satguru, 1991) for some interesting discussion on time.

Language possesses a number of expressions denoting time-relation: simultaneity, subsequence, precedence, etc. Moreover, with the help of suffixes, it can express time and time aspects of action, viz. *kriyate, kṛtām, kariṣyati,* etc. The first example indicates (through the suffix *te*) present which is in continuation. The second (with the help of the suffix *kṛta*) indicates past activity and the third indicates future time (with the help of the suffix *sya+te*). We make efficacious use of these expressions in our everyday experience and there exists, subsequently, an empirical applicability (*vyavahāra*) of these expressions which would not be possible were they based on fiction.

In communication, language acts as an agent of description. To provide a correct description of an event or action so as to make it understandable, it is necessary to place it in a time perspective. This is where language depicts time: past, present and future.

In order to represent the timeline of an action or event, many languages have certain commonly accepted norms. The grammar of such languages contains these norms. In order to project time, grammar sets down various rules that deal with tense, mood, etc. For instance, the three categories of time that we encounter in our life, namely, past, present and future, are expressed by certain grammatical elements.

In the context of the Indian grammatical tradition, time is internalized in the principle of *bhāva pradhānatā* or the fundamentality of verbal meaning and rules for handling temporal contents of sentences. The other point that is highlighted is time as a *śakti* (*kālaśakti*) or power of *Śabda-Brahman* (word as the Ultimate Principle). In this chapter we shall focus on the former aspect of time.

In grammatical analysis the concept of time plays an

important role in explaining the formulation of verbal derivatives. Let us look at the diagram given below to find how a sentence — which is the basic indivisible unit — can be analysed according to Indian grammarians.

Rāmaḥ		**Grāman**		**Gacchati**	
Rāma	Su	Grāma	Am		
(*Pratipadika*)	(Nominal Case suffix)	(Nominal root)	(Accusative Case suffix)	*Gam* (Verbal root)	*Tip* (Verbal suffix)

Kartṛ (Agent)	*Pratham Puruṣa* 3rd person)	*Ekavacana* (singular)	*Vartamāna kāla* (Present tense)

Thus, from the illustration above we know how time is internalized as a linguistic unit in a sentence. There are other examples too. Other than the suffix indicated above, there are also some *kṛt* suffixes which express time.

When an action appears through verbs in a temporal order, it is called verbal time. The above sentence is an illustration. In examples like *gacchati, gamiṣyati,* etc. through verbal suffixes, different time variations like *vartamāna* (present), and *bhaviṣyat* (future) are indicated.

Another type of suffix expressing time is *kṛdanta*. When time is understood from nouns derived from roots, such as *gatavān, gataḥ, pacan, kriyamāna,* etc. they are called *kṛdanta*.

In Sanskrit we can realize the sense of time in various ways. Given below is a list of eleven examples each of which represents a category. We shall take them up for discussion below.

1. *Rāmaḥ grāmam gachhati* (Rāma goes to the village)
2. *He rāma! Atrāgaccha* (O Rāma! Come here)

3. *Ete grāma gatāḥ* (These people have gone to their village)
4. *Bhabhatā yastavyam* (you have to perform *yoga* in its proper time)
5. *Bhavān yatatām* (do perform *yoga* in its proper time)
6. *Māsam āste* (he stays for a whole month)
7. *Vasan dadarśa* (living there he saw)
8. *Gacchati sma/ Puā asti* (he was going/there was)
9. *Bhūto gataḥ/Bhūta sattā* (the jar is past/existence existed)
10. *Satvaram gṛham Āgaccha/ ciram jīvatu* (come home quickly/wish you long life)
11. *Kālo madhu* (This is the spring of time)

We have already discussed the first category of sentence. In the second category the emphasis is laid upon the length of time required to pronounce a *pluta* (protracted sound). Similarly, it can be realized in case of long (*dīrgha*) and short (*hrasva*) vowels too. The time requirement to pronounce a phoneme is called *mātrā*. The short, the long and the protracted vowels require one, two and three *mātrā*s respectively. There is also a half-vowel which requires an *ardhamātrā*. These different measurements of different phonemes are compared with activities and phenomena in nature in the Sanskrit tradition. For instance, the *ardhamātrā* is the time taken for the wink of an eye, the flash of lightning or the peck of a woodpecker. A short vowel's time is equal to the time required for the chirping of a sparrow; a long vowel's duration is the time required for the crow of a crow, and the duration of a protracted vowel is equal to the time taken for a peacock's call. These short, long and protracted vowels do not really point to time relation but are themselves determined by time.

In the third category of sentences, the underlined words are the nouns derived from roots and are called *kṛdanta*s. The *kṛdantas* are words ending with *kṛt* suffixes. Among the *kṛt* suffixes there are certain suffixes which give the sense of something done in the past time, some give the idea of an activity in the present and some others give the idea of time in the future. In the quoted examples, all the three *kṛdanta* suffixes indicate past.

In the fourth category of sentences such as *bhavatā yaṣṭavyam*, the word *yaṣṭavyam* also gives the sense of time. The suffix *tavya* gives the idea of proper time, apart from its usually meaning.

In the fifth category of sentences, such as *bhavān yajatām*, the *loṭ* is used in the sense of "proper time" as an additional meaning to its usual meaning. Thereby, the meaning derived is, "you should perform sacrifice in proper time."

In the sixth category of sentences, the period of time becomes the grammatical object of a verb. Thereby, it gives the idea that his stay covers a period of one month.

In the seventh category of sentence, a typical syntactical agreement is found between the two words expressing two different times. In the sentence *vasan dadarśa* the word *vasan* expresses present time whereas *dadarśa* gives the idea of past and, yet, there is a syntactical agreement between the two and, hence, the whole sentence gives the idea of past since *dadarśa* is considered as the chief expressive of time (*mukhyakriyākāla*).

In the eighth category, the sense of time is expressed through different terms such as, *sma*, *purā*, etc. which give the idea of past time. In association with these terms, verbal forms such as *gacchati*, *karoti*, etc. which are otherwise in present, give the sense of past.

In case of the ninth category, the activity called existence, which is denoted by the verbal root, *bhū*, is made known to have become past through the affix *kta*. Here, existence is inherently connected with the past, but there is no direct relation between the substance and time. In the second illustration (*bhūta sattā*), the *sattā* is expressed by the root in the form of action and the meaning expressed by the word *sattā* is in the form of a substance. Thus, the pastness of the latter is understood through the pastness of the former. Hence, there is no inconsistency in the understanding of time element in case of these complex sentences.

In the tenth category, the time expressives are independent of grammatical analysis and they express the idea of different limits of time, relative terms of time, etc.

In the last category of sentences, time expressions such as *kālaḥ*, *samayaḥ*, etc. in a sentence help to determine the meaning from different polysymic words. For example, in the given example, the word *madhu* is understood in the sense of "spring" since it is used in the context of *kāla*.

Apart from the above illustrations, there are some other illuminations where time sense is realised through the relating speed of speech of different speakers, such as *drut* (fast), *madhya* (medium) and *lambita* (stretched or prolonged). This corresponds to time realization through *hrasva*, *dīrgha*, etc. but at a different level.

In the above discussion, I have briefly pointed as to how time is realized through the different uses of language. Thus, I have considered how time affects language or how the notion of time governs language. This aspect of time is considered the grammatical aspect of time. The other aspect of time in Indian grammatical tradition is the metaphysical dimension where time is considered as a power (*kālaśakti*). It is the Bhartṛharian school which mainly deals with this aspect of time and has not been discussed here.

5

Time in Indian Spiritual Traditions and its Representation in Indian Poetry

Niranjan Mohanty

IN this article an attempt is made to look into the concept of time as developed in the Indian traditions — the traditions which have given Indian culture a composite rhythm, a rhythm which is unique and distinctive. This article tries to suggest that time has acquired significance partly because of its all-comprehensive nature, and partly because of its insistence on the possibilities of binaries. The concepts of time gather importance and meaning in the context of the autonomous construction of binaries such as Time/time, eternal/temporal, timeless/time, construction/destruction, good/evil, spiritual/physical (or material). And to my mind, precisely because of such infinite variables in terms of binaries, time has proved to be baffling and confounding more than clarifying in clear-cut terms.

Time has been variously viewed as a substance, single, omnipresent, permanent, or the measure or dimension of things possessing movement. It is also the cause of the origin, maintenance, and destruction of objects. It is the thread-holder of the world. Actualization of power is generated by time, so that birth, growth, decay and extinction of things/objects/

beings depend entirely on time. Time is the very self (*ātman*) or essence of everything.[1] It is operation or movement itself. Time, therefore, is instrumental to the manifestation of an activity or a series of activities, divinely oriented. Time is the engineer of cycles. It makes the universe assume a sequence. Time has also been represented by past, present and future as its powers.[2] In themselves they do not contain a sequence but engender sequence on the objects. It has also been argued that time has only two powers, which are responsible for appearance and disappearance. Time is one of the seminal powers of *Brahman*. *Brahman* is bereft of any sequence. But it can be realized through the sequence of temporality. Therefore, the primary function of time is to present phenomena in a temporal sequence so as ultimately to lead to the origin of time, i.e. the *Brahman*.

Time as the power of the *Brahman* or God makes him the creator and the destroyer both. Arjuna declines to hold weapons and fight against his brothers, teachers and near and dear ones. Kṛṣṇa (the *avatāra*) explains to him the essence of his own self and the essence of the universe that he created. In order to comprehend the vision of the Godhead, the latter sanctions special insight to Arjuna with which he beholds the

---

1. This is the view held by Bhartṛhari (CE 450–510), the Indian Grammarian and philosopher.

   For a full discussion on Bhartṛhari's concept of time, see, *Encyclopedia of Indian Philosophies: The Philosophy of the Grammarians*, vol. V, ed. Harold G. Coward & K. Kunjunni Raja (Delhi: Motilal Banarsidass) 1990, pp 169–70.

2. Bhartṛhari makes a mention of two kinds of past, two kinds of present and four kinds of future. *Encyclopedia of Indian Philosophies*. vol. V, p. 170.

   Time is also the *svatontryasakti* (power of complete freedom) of the *Brahman*, Bhartṛhari argues. *Encyclopedia of Indian Philosophies*, vol. V, p. 196; also see *New Encyclopedia Britannica*, vol. 28, 15th edn. (Chicago, 1987), p. 654.

essence of the self. Sri Aurobindo in a chapter "The Vision of the World-spirit — Time, the Destroyer" from *Essays on the Gītā* (1970, 1993), sums up the essence of Indian spirituality *vis-à-vis* the concept of time:

> Indian spirituality knows that God is Love and Peace and Calm and Eternity — the *Gītā* which presents us with these terrible images, speaks of the Godhead who embodies himself in them as the lover and friend of all creatures. But there is too the sterner aspect of his divine government of the world which meets us from the beginning, the aspect of destruction, and to ignore it is to miss the full reality of the divine Love and Peace and Calm and Eternity and even to throw on it an aspect of partiality and illusion, because the comforting exclusive form in which it is put is not borne by the nature of the world in which we live.[3]

God is both the creator and the destroyer. When Arjuna wanted to know the working of God's will, Lord Kṛṣṇa replied:

> Destruction . . . is the will of my working with which I stand here in this field of Kurukṣetra, the field of the working out of the *dharma*, the field of human action, [as we might symbolically translate the descriptive phrase, *dharma kṣetra kurukṣetre*] a worldwide destruction which has come in the process of Time-spirit. . . . I as Time have to destroy the old structures and to build up a new, mighty and splendid Kingdom. Thou art a human instrument of the divine Power and Wisdom, in this struggle which thou cannot prevent, to battle for the right and slay and conquer its opponents. Thou too, the human soul in Nature, hast to enjoy in Nature the fruit given by Me, the empire of right and justice.[4]

---

3. Sri Aurobindo, *Essays on the Gītā* (Pondicherry: Sri Aurobindo Ashram, 1970), p. 267.

4. Ibid., p. 367.

From this dialogue and answer, at least one thing is clear. First, that nothing can happen on earth without the divine Will, and secondly, that God as Time is the arbiter of his supreme-governance and thirdly, that God as Time is responsible for destruction, for the sake of creation of a new order and its preservation. From the explanation quoted above, it is further evident that Godhead himself creates a set of binaries, such as God/human, eternal/temporal. While constructing this set of binaries, God legitimizes a privileged status for himself. This binary, once again, results in another set of binaries, such as superior/inferior, permanent/impermanent, unchanging/changing. I believe the Indian spiritual discourses and texts have posited this complex set of binaries with a view to creating a sense of fear and awe so that the parameters of privileging can possibly lead to, theoreticians would say, colonizer/colonized, I/the other, centre/margin — a set of new binaries. Had not God explained his position as the saviour/the creator and preserver of the creation, He would have appeared as a tyrannical colonizer. Godhead explained to Arjuna:

> "I am Time the Destroyer of beings" does not mean either that he is the Time-Spirit alone or that the whole essence of the Time-Spirit is destruction. But it is this which is the present will of his workings, *pravṛtti*. Destruction is always a simultaneous or alternate element which keeps pace with creation and it is by destroying and renewing that the Master of Life does long work of preservation. Moreover, destruction is the first condition of progress.[5]

---

5. Yin-Yang principle in China evidences the cyclic view of time. According to the Chinese concept, the alteration between Yin, the passive female principle, and Yang the dynamic Male principle results in the cyclic view of time. "When either Yin or Yang goes to extremes, it overlaps the other principle, which is its correlative →

Thus, ultimately one comes across the primary motif of God, i.e. progress, obviously, human progress. I believe, this single acknowledgement of the God saves him from being the political colonizer of the human world. One aspect of Indian spiritual traditions which appears to be baffling to me is the location or position of the Divine Self. It has been perceived that this self is at the centre of the human world, and hence, all human actions lead but to this centre. This, centrifugality of human actions is possibly responsible for the creation of the Time eternal. Once again, this Divine Self is above the human world and creates a centre for itself in the Universe. To my mind, the problem arises when we put God at two centres. Indian philosophers and torchbearers of Indian spirituality advocate that the mortal/human is indescribably related to and ordained by these two centres, even if the temporal world, the sequential and materialistic, scientific world posits man at the centre of his own temporal world as the privileged being. This willing allegiance to and acceptance of the God at the centre of the human world is because of the peculiar nature of the Indian mind or the Indian mindset. One is reminded of what Ramranjan Mukherjee in a perceptive paper observes:

→ and complement in consequence of being its opposite. In the philosophy of Empedocles, an early Greek thinker, the equivalents of Yin and Yang were Love and Strife. Empedocles revolted against the denial of the reality of motion and plurality that was made by his Eleatic predecessors on the strength of mere logic. He broke up the Eleatics' motionless, and therefore, timeless, unitary reality into a movement of four elements that were alternately harmonized by Love and set at variance by Strife. Empedocle's Love and Strife, Like Yin and Yang, each overlapped the other when they had gone to extremes." *New Encyclopedia Britannica*, vol. 28, p. 654. Also see Aurobindo, *Essays on the Gītā*, p. 370.

> Indian mind thus conceives the universe as a single unfragmented whole, engulfed by the one Absolute and repeatedly asserts that, in fragmentation lies ugliness, while in unity is enshrined charmingness; in fragmentation there is restlessness and consequential death, while unity ushers in complete repose and immortality. When the one is fragmented and is seen as such, man feels himself alienated from the stream of Universal life, as a result of which he feels himself small and a stranger to his association of universe. It is not without reason, therefore, that Indian philosophy in all its systems describes the one Infinite as the culmination of all Philosophies — Indian art regards presentation of the one complete whole as the terminal point of all forms of art — and Indian literature also in its endeavour to establish itself as grand and sublime reflects the immeasurable Infinite in its small compass the complete man, resplendent in the light of his multicoloured personality as its hero.[6]

An individual experiences changes in the time-flow. The sum total of all these changes that an individual experiences is nothing but the perception of the reality. These changes also get repeated, for example, as the change of season. Possibly this runs quite parallel to the view held by Indian spiritual traditions that *avatāra*s of Hindu god Viṣṇu appear on the earth to save it from the corruptive, tyrannical forces of evil. The *avatāra*s appear to safeguard the good and preserve it, destroying the evil. It is, therefore, convenient to perceive the fact that because of such repetitive manifestations of God on the earth, time contains a cyclical order. But the Christians believe that the incarnation of God in Jesus was a unique event and it never got repeated and Christianity held time as a one-

6. Ramranjan Mukherjee, "Indianness in Ancient Indian Poetry", *Literature and Criticism*, vol. 2, no. 1 (April 2002), p. 17.

way flow and not as a cyclic one. This one-way flow of time allows the Western thinkers to conceive of the idea of maker or creator or law-giver of time at whose command the beginning and the end of time-flow is ordained. Some thinkers have felt that such limits can be imagined only if there is some timeless power that has set time going and intends or is set to stop it. A god, who creates and then annihilates time, if he is held to be omnipotent, is often credited with having done this with a benevolent purpose that is being carried out according to plan. The omnipotent God's plan, in this view, governs this time-flow and is made manifest to humans in progressive revelations through the prophets — from Abraham, by way of Moses, Isaiah and Jesus, to the Prophet Muhammad (as Muslims believe).[7]

It is interesting to see now that whether one accepts the cyclic view of time or the linear, progressive view of time, the one representing the East and the other the West, both accept God or a timeless power as the maker, creator, or governor of time. And by such acceptance both views abide by the construction of the primary set of binaries, i.e. timeless/time. One can also relate what Lord Kr̥ṣṇa told Arjuna at the battlefield when the latter declined to fight against his near and dear ones. Thus, both the views accept the invulnerability, the infalliability of the Master's plan, and thereby the mystery and grandeur of the Master plan, i.e. to protect good and tarnish evil, to purify the earth that has been burdened by evil, whether it is through Kurukṣetra or through the "Ah!" of Christ on the cross. God, the maker of time and space and the chief architect of the Master Plan (i.e. creation) remains invincible, incomprehensible, undecipherable colonizer, governed by benevolence and not by mere willingness to civilize the barbarians. In God, the timeless spirit, there is a

7. Ramranjan Mukherjee, "Indianness in Ancient Indian Poetry."

different kind of colonizer, a redeemer of burdens of pain and mortality and he is Timeless. His colonizing effects save us from the burdens of mortality and reality and drag us towards that centre or space which is timeless, which represents the eternal Time.

If we look into the *Rāmāyaṇa* we encounter a similar Master plan of the maker. In the archetypical fight between good, represented by Rāma (an *avatāra*), and evil, represented by Rāvaṇa, it is the good that establishes its victory over evil, and thus Rāma, the divinely appointed human, becomes instrumental in the preservation and perpetuation of the forces of good. There are instances of Dūrgā — the *Śakti* incarnate overpowering Mahiṣāsura — of Viṣṇu terminating devotee Prahalāda's father Hiraṇyakaśyipu, the incarnate of evil. To my mind, it is the cyclical ordinance of time that has rendered possible this continuous purging off of the world, leading towards a sense of harmony between the time and the timeless.

Speculations regarding time formed an essential part of a particular Indian philosophy known as the *Kālavāda*. G.J. Whitrow's observations may be of certain relevance:

> The term *kāla* was originally employed by the Hindus in the *Ṛgveda* to denote the "right moment" in connection with sacrificial ritual. Later it came to denote "time" generally, and it was usually employed in that sense in Sanskrit writings. In the Vedic period the abstract idea of time was regarded as the fundamental principle of the universe, but whether it was made into a deity is uncertain. The word *kāla* has been associated, however, with Kāli, "the Black One," one of the forms of the consort of the god Śiva. Time was regarded as black and connected with Śiva, god of destruction, because it is hard and pitiless.[8]

8. G.T. Whitrow, *Time in History* (New York: Oxford University Press, 1988), pp. 87-88.

II

In the second part of this paper, I would like to illustrate how two Indian poets — Sālabega, a seventeenth-century Oriyā devotional poet, and A.K. Ramanujan, a twentieth-century Indian English poet — tried to perpetuate the binary, such as timeless/time, or immortal/mortal, or spiritual/material which lies at the core of their understanding of self, body and the outside world of reality — all governed by time. This, I believe, is how the poets comprehend, reconstruct and represent Indian culture and try to come to terms with their perceptions of time (both the eternal and the temporal).

Sālabega was the son of a Brāhmaṇa widow and a Muslim Subedar, Lal Beg. He was drawn towards Hindu *bhakti mārga* by the influence of his mother. Sālabega, wounded in a battle, writhing in pain and despite royal care, could not recover. At the advice of the mother he offered his prayers to Lord Kṛṣṇa. On the 7th day he had a dream in which Lord Kṛṣṇa offered him *vibhūti* and asked him to use the same on the wound. He got relief and the wound healed. He ran to his mother to narrate this miraculous tale of recovery because of his devotion and prayer. Subsequently he came to know that Lord Jagannāth of Purī is none other than Lord Kṛṣṇa. He devoted the rest of his life to composing prayer-songs on Kṛṣṇa and Lord Jagannāth. His prayer songs are enriched not only by devotional integrity but also by intense metaphoric quality. The cure by God's mercy made him infinitely indebted to him and because of such indebtedness he considers himself low, mortal, falliable, and God, high, infalliable, and immortal. Sālabega constructs this set of binaries — quite in harmony with the spiritual traditions of India — and treats himself as time-tethered, mortal, and tiny and God as immortal, timeless, pure, Love. I am tempted to assume that Indian spiritual traditions are responsible for the construction of such binaries, as divine/human, timeless/time, spiritual/material, immortal/mortal. Sālabega's poems don't bear titles, but in the concluding part of each poem his name figures. There is a deliberate attempt at marginalizing his own name and self, and representing his own self as trite and jejune as he was "*Javana*" (a Muslim) and a mortal. Such willing marginalization of the self is the manifestation of a sense of humility and devotional sincerity. Sālabega's sense of humility gets at once articulated, when he sings:

> O! my dark-and-round-eyed Lord,
> O! my contrite heart's dark diamond,
> Not even once did you intently reveal
> Your miraculous manifestation!
> I know, I'm not worthy, I'm trite.
> Let this useless being wither away
> At your lotus-feet, O! Lord! . . .
> You adorn your crown with a twig
> of a jungle's blackberry. Let my tired soul
> take shelter at thy feet O! Lord Jagannātha,
> thus sings Sālabega, the low-born.[9]

Even in another poem Sālabega willingly privileges Lord Kṛṣṇa and Rādhā — the immortal pair:

> Perhaps, there's no salvation without chanting
> The honeyed names of Rādhā-Kṛṣṇa,
> Thus sings Salabega, the low-born.[10]

In another poem Sālabega harps on the binary of the mortal and the immortal, the former to be redeemed by the latter:

9. Niranjan Mohanty, *Salabega : A Monograph* (Delhi: Sahitya Akademi, 1996) p.92.

10. Ibid., p. 93.

The cunning and shrewd Lord, weaves
a fence around you, binding you to ties
and bondages. You only rear a golden parrot
in the clayey cage of your body.

The parrot will not stay,
surely, it'll fly away. No other hope
for me, no other go, except those lotus feet
of the Lord; thus sings Salabega, the low-born.[11]

Elsewhere he prays:

Let my contrite soul
wither away at the feet
of Rādhā-Kr̥ṣṇa,
thus sings Salabega, the low-born.[12]

The willingness to be united with Lord, the Timeless, and to free himself from the burdens of binaries and reality, remains at the centre of Sālabega's devotional poems. I quote here another short poem:

If I'm alive
I shall visit Br̥ndāban.
In my own eyes
I shall see Śrī Madhusūdana.
I shall have my bath
In Śyāmakuṇḍa and Rohiṇīkuṇḍa
and consecrate my being.
Round and round I shall go
Round and round I would visit
the lofty rock Govardhana.
Gleefully I'd drink water
from the Yamunā.

11. Niranjan Mohanty, op. cit., p. 89.

12. Ibid., p. 108.

> I'd sing there the glories
> of the Lord and the means
> to our salvation.
> Plucking dust from the place
> where Rādhā and Kṛṣṇa make love,
> I shall adorn my body.
> I shall sleep beneath creepers
> and bushes, and dream of my Lord.[13]

I am reminded of Rabindranath Tagore's *Gītāñjali* wherein one discovers the amalgamation of humility and devotional integrity, and the construction of the binaries which privilege the Immortal over the mortal.

If Sālabega's God, the Timeless One is distant and occupies a higher pedestal, Tagore's god is much more human. The poet's devotion and sincerity are compellingly instrumental to humanizing his god. Tagore constructs a more reciprocatory bond between himself and his god, without violating the privileged position of God. In the beginning of *Gītāñjali*, Tagore represents his own self/body as a "frail vessel" but at the same time he recognizes the worth of this frail vessel at the touch of the hands of the timeless:

> At the immortal touch of thy hands my
> little heart loses its limits in joy and gives
> birth to utterance ineffable.[14]

Tagore treats his heart as "beggarly" (verse 22), "arid" (verse 23), and he himself as "poverty-stricken" (verse 24), and God as the king, the "King of Kings" (verse 31) — the king who comes down from his throne and stands at the poet's cottage door. Thus, in Tagore we find another kind of binary, i.e.

---

13. Niranjan Mohanty, op. cit., p. 108.

14. Rabindranath Tagore, *Gītāñjali* (Delhi: Macmillan India Ltd., 1991) verse 1.

king/beggar. But this binary gets dissolved, once the union takes place:

> In my life thy will is
> ever taking shape.
> And for this, thou who art the king
> of kings hast decked thyself in beauty
> to captivate my heart. And for this thy love
> loses itself in the love of thy lover,
> and there art thou seen in the perfect
> union of two.[15]

Tagore treats God, the timeless as the Lover with whom he intends to meet in the solitude of night. Yet Tagore is conscious of his mortality, of his identity as being temporal:

> I know that the day will come when my
> sight of this earth shall be lost, and life
> will take its leave in silence, drawing the
> last curtain over my eyes. . . .
>
> When I think of this end of my moments,
> the barrier of the moments
> breaks and I see by the light of death thy
> World with its carelesss treasures.[16]

And once again, Tagore constructs the binary and breaks it in the concluding section of the poem:

> In one salutation to thee, my God, let
> all my senses spread out and touch this
> world at thy feet. . . .
>
> Like a flock of homesick cranes flying
> night and day back to their mountain
> nests let all my life take its voyage to its

15. Rabindranath Tagore, op. cit., verse 37.

16. Ibid., verse 61.

eternal home in one salutation to thee.[17]

Gītānjali thus celebrates the essence of Indian spiritual traditions, without failing to celebrate what is temporal, earthly, physical, or what is in time.

A.K. Ramanujan who lived and died in the U.S. left behind a large body of his writings, including translations from the classical Kannaḍa poetry. He is one of the major voices of Indian poetry in English. He was the first to think of and advocate for the formation of an indigenous tradition of Indian poetry in English, by making use of the resources of native or regional literatures. Even if he lived in the U.S., Ramanujan remains an instinctive insider. Ramanujan, towards the fag end of his creative career, seems to have constructed the kind of binary, such as immortal/mortal, eternal/temporal, which is the influence of his understanding of the Indian spiritual traditions. Even if his poetry has been instrumental in the celebration of the body, the temporal, the time-oriented being, Ramanujan recognizes the significance of the process of birth, growth, decay and extinction which is the direct product of the temporal time that signifies our sense of mortality. In "Elements of Composition" the point of realization comes full circle with the concluding image:

And even as I add,
I lose, decompose
Into my elements,
Into other names and forms,

Past, and passing, tenses
without time,
caterpillar on a leaf, eating
being eaten.[18]

---

17. Rabindranath Tagore, op. cit., verse 68.

18. A.K. Ramanujan, *The Collected Poems* (Delhi: Oxford University Press, 1995), p. 121.

In another poem "Death and the Good Citizen" Ramanujan contrasts between the Hindu and the Western ways of cremation. He recognizes the fact that life ends in death, and that our sense of mortality has to accept death as the ultimate end:

> But
> You know my tribe, incarnate
> they'll speak proverbs, contest
> my will, against such degradation.
> Hidebound, even worms cannot
> have me: they'll cremate
> me in Sanskrit and sandalwood,
> have me sterilized
> to a scatter of ash.[19]

In "Mythologies 1" Ramanujan reiterates the binary such as time/timeless, physical/spiritual, privileging the latter over the former. The poem is suggestive of the Child Kṛṣṇa-Pūtanā myth, in which the demon experiences death and is redeemed. More than the representation of the myth what is important and meaningful is the poet's prayer:

> O Terror with a baby face,
> suck me dry. Drink my venom
> Renew my breath.[20]

In "Mythologies 2" the poet uses the myth of Hiraṇyakaśyipu, who was tarnished by Viṣṇu in his Narasiṁha *avatāra*. But the last line of the poem reveals the poet's anxiety to be redeemed:

> . . . slay now my faith in doubt,
> End my commerce with bat and night-owl.
> Adjust my single eye, rainbow bubble,

19. A.K. Ramanujan, op. cit., p. 131.

20. Ibid., p. 221.

so I too may see all things double.[21]

Ramanujan, by revisiting these myths, is not only able to establish a connection between the past and the present but also to celebrate his identity as an Indian being the product of that spiritual tradition which privileges the Timeless over time, the eternal over the temporal. Construction of such binaries in the Indian spiritual traditions and their representations in literature makes it clear that even if they posit an independence, they are mutually inclusive and because of this inclusive tendency become both meaningful and significant. I believe Indian spiritual traditions, while constructing such binaries, aim at achieving this purpose.

---

21. A.K. Ramanujan, op. cit., p. 226.

6

Time in the Indian Traditions

A Note on the Mahābhārata[1]

Binda Paranjape

I

ONCE, a traveller got down at a village bus stop. He asked the first villager he saw, "How much time would it take to reach Mukundapur?" There was no reply. The question was repeated but still there was no response. The traveller thought that his question has reached a deaf ear and hence thought it wise to start walking towards his desired destination. After a while he heard the villager shouting from behind, "It will take you half a day to reach Mukundpur." The traveller asked in astonishment, "why didn't you tell me when I asked you?" The villager replied, "How was I supposed to answer you when I did not know how fast you walk?" In the practical day-to-day life of an average Indian such a scientific understanding of time (time in relation to movement and speed) is, however, absent. For the majority of Indians,

1. The following readings have been useful in writing this paper: G.S. Herbert, *Time: A Metaphysical Study* (Trivandram: College Book House, 1978); Romila Thapar, *Ancient Indian Social History: Some Interpretations* (Delhi: Orient and Longman Ltd., 1978); Cornelia Dimmitt and J.A.B. van Buitenen, *Classical Hindu Mythology: A Reader in Sanskrit Puranas* (Delhi: Indian Book Centre, 1998); Romila Thapar, *History and Beyond* (Delhi: Oxford University Press, 2000).

especially the villagers, watches are still just items of luxury than tools of utility. Life moves along the normal course from childhood to old age without being measured in terms of calendar time. The only events that need to have a tag of dateable time are births of children. Even that datability is far removed from the standard calendar dates universally applied.[2] Women associate their menstruation cycles with the position of moon, that too with more evident positions like full moon or new moon. Accordingly, the fertilization time is guessed.[3] The birth of a child is noted by the position of the moon, and the season. But rarely does one keep a record of his or her exact age. This is obvious when half of the population is still illiterate. However this does not mean Indian folks do not have any perception of time. They understand time mainly through the process of fertility, reproduction and rejuvenation. For them time means time to sow seeds, reap the harvest, prepare the soil for cultivation and many more such activities. The birth of their child is often associated with some cultivation activity or even the birth of a calf and the birth of a child can become reference to each other. There is perfect harmony between their lives and the nature around them.

II

What exactly then is the perception of time of Indians by and large? Time with the capital letter "T" was not a part of

---

2. Usually village brāhmaṇa (priest) works also as an astrologer who prepares horoscope for the newborn. Since in majority of the cases the parents are illiterate the horoscope remains unread forever. Making of the horoscope is also for a privileged few. A large number of Indians are away even from this much piece of time reckoning.

3. My mother worked as a village health worker. She had to register women for the antenatal and post-natal care programme. This was her experience and it is still the case — that is what I hear.

everyday life of Indians till recently, neither was time divided into meticulously counted segments like minutes and hours except for a few learned Indians like Āryabhaṭṭa, Bhāskarācārya and the like in astronomy and hence in the field of time-space research.[4] But for common Indians the immediate reference to time came through the position of moon which they could actually see or through unusual phenomena like eclipses. Otherwise time *per se* was not a subject of deliberation at a conscious level. The tradition has continued even today.

The general perception of time of Indians is largely shaped by the popular tradition of Itihāsa-Purāṇa.[5] This tradition propagated the idea of mythical time. Thus, all humanly impossible ranges of time were allocated to gods and mythical heroes. The time reckoning of gods was easily accepted to be of a much higher proportion than human beings even can think of.[6] While a standard lifespan of a human being was believed to be of hundred years (a stereotyped expression, without any scientific testimony) the lives of the mythical heroes and of seers were easily of thousands of years[7] and of gods in multiples of thousands and millions. All these were told to the generations of masses without being questioned or doubt being raised regarding these myths. There appears to have been a perfect understanding between the story-teller and the listener. Thus as in case of all primitive cultures, the Indians also understood the metaphorical cliché "long long ago"

4. Also see G.S. Herbert, *Indian Philosophy* (1978), p. 177.
5. S. Bhattacharya and Romila Thapar (eds.), *Situating Indian History* (Delhi, 1986), pp. 353-83.
6. J. Mckin Malville, *Time and Eternal Change,* New Delhi: Indira Gandhi National Centre for the Arts, 1990, p. 92.
7. Ādiparva, *Mahābhārata.*

instantaneously and did not ask questions like "How much time has lapsed since?" Mythological time is the time of gods, sages and ancient heroes. Their existence was a fact of a very high antiquity and we, the mortals, bound by a lifespan of a few years (hundred) were not supposed to question it.

According to the practical wisdom of common people, time was the process of age and decay ultimately resulting in the cessation of life. In other words time meant death.[8] Time is also understood as healer. Apparently these two perceptions are contradictory to each other. However, deep down, the common Indian understands that the death or the blessing of life given by the healer are not matters of their choice. The Time that heals the scars assuring the continuity and the Time that causes the cessation of life are in a way the same.[9]

III

In the process of civilization human beings acquired the skill of recording the mental abstractions of collective experiences which formed the core of human wisdom. Another skill which was equally important was the skill of transmitting that wisdom from generation to generation. Both these processes are constantly active and they represent the ceaseless quest for knowledge of human beings (human beings as of having a collective identity). "Time" always has been one of the subjects of this process. Indians seem to have taken long strides towards the ultimate understanding of "Time," i.e. in relation to space and the self. This is evident from a large mass of literature produced by Indians over a period of hundreds of years. It is not just a matter of anthropological or sociological observation that the Indians are by and large far away from

8. Time which is literally translated as *kāla* is used as a synonym to death. *Mahābhārata*, VI.60.58 and also XII.149.9.

9. *Mahābhārata*, III.57.1.

the mechanical mathematics of time. Much more pertinent would be a probe into the question, why so? What has been there in the collective consciousness of the Indians regarding time? To make a beginning towards the understanding of the Indian concept of time one can look into the rich treasure of literature composed, preserved and transmitted from generation to generation of Indians. What appears to be a poetic narrative at the first encounter, in many cases, turns out to be having a potential for philosophy and practical wisdom. A note on the *Mahābhārata* is presented here in this context.

IV

The *Mahābhārata* is a significant example of the Itihāsa-Purāṇa tradition of Indians. This text is like an encyclopedia of Indian culture which embodies knowledge of generations of Indians with regard to Nature, Mind, Soul, Universe or the threefold reality (Space, Time and Soul). It makes a proud claim that whatever is embodied in this epic may be found elsewhere but it is impossible to find anywhere else that which is not there in this epic.[10] The text is believed to have undergone three phases of composition. The first is supposed to be by Vyāsa and it was called Itihāsa with a particular title *Jaya*. It was modified and enlarged by Vaiśampāyana with a title *Bhārata*. The third compilation was done by Sauti and being the largest it was called the *Mahābhārata*.

The *Mahābhārata* is primarily a biological narrative of the lives of warrior heroes ultimately establishing a faith that righteousness wins over evil. While doing so the text has successfully incorporated into its main body some of the extremely complex subjects of human deliberation. It also poses questions which the entire humanity has been asking

10. *Mahābhārata*, I.56.33.

for generations together and gives answers which at least create a hope of end of certain quests. One such question is regarding life beyond birth and death. Is there something beyond death or was there some thing before birth? In other words, the force that takes one from birth to death, is it existent before and after? The perception of time in the *Mahābhārata* can be contextualized through this inquiry.

The author of the *Mahābhārata* can be taken as the first case towards the understanding of certain perceptions of time. Vyāsa, biologically born to Satyavatī and Parāśara is the author of this text. He is constantly referred to as the seer and the knower of the Vedas (the ultimate knowledge). The legitimacy of his authorship of the text partly comes from the maternal lineage and partly from his parenthood of Pāṇḍu, Dhṛtarāṣṭra and Vidura.[11] Interestingly enough he is considered to be the right person to narrate the Itihāsa also because he has the knowledge of the three times — past, present and future. Vyāsa's role in the epic is almost over after he procreated the children to the widows of the Kuru family.[12] He is not expected to father these children in the social sense. However Vyāsa is everywhere. He has seen it all and since he is deathless he will see all that will happen. One then wonders, what is he? Is he a human? If so, how is he deathless?[13] What would be the

11. The main characters of the *Mahābhārata*, viz. the Pāṇḍavas and Kauravas were the children of Pāṇḍu and Dhṛtarāṣṭra. *Mahābhārata*, I.306.

12. Vyāsa produced children to Satyavatī's daughters-in-law who were childless widows. This was legitimate according to the tradition of *niyoga*. According to this tradition the childless widows can beget children from their brother-in-law. Vyāsa was the brother-in-law of Satyavatī's daughters-in-law, viz. Ambikā and Ambālikā.

13. In the *Mahābhārata* there is no mention of any particular event when he got the boon of immortality. Vyāsa's immortality is →

meaning of his existence after he procreated those children in the context of the *Mahābhārata*? Vyāsa in the *Mahābhārata* is wisdom incarnate. That is his inborn quality and his wisdom cannot be transferred to anybody else or as he himself puts it, "By raising my hands I am telling the truth but hardly any one listens to it."[14] In that case the question of the purpose of Vyāsa's immortality becomes more complex. For what purpose will he live? Vyāsa, it seems, stands for the hope of human beings of conquering death. His deathlessness represents the eternal human dream of conquering time which causes decay and death. Time is death, death is a new beginning but the humans are sceptical about this new beginning because it is without the support of the gross elements of body. Hence what one desires is to live forever in this bodily form. Vyāsa is a referent to the mortality of the other human beings.[15]

Vyāsa's immortality represents one dimension of the perception of time in the *Mahābhārata*. One more dimension of this perception comes through the character of Bhīṣma. Bhīṣma received from his father the boon of postponing his death as long as he wished.[16] At this point an obvious question comes

---

→ highlighted by the popular Purāṇic mythology. It is believed that in every *yuga* Vyāsa is born as a part of the total creation. This myth is supported by the *Mahābhārata* where there is no mention of Vyāsa's death. In one episode, when his son Śuka parted with this world and went to heaven in his human form, Vyāsa, out of grief, thought of renouncing the world completely. At this point Rudra consoled him and brought him back to the active life. (*Mahābhārata*, Śāntiparva).

14. *Mahābhārata*, XVIII.5.49.

15. The tradition believes that there are seven *cirañjīvas* literally meaning immortals, viz. Aśvatthāmā, Bali, Vyāsa, Hanumān, Vibhīṣaṇa, Kṛpa and Paraśurāma. Out of these seven Aśvatthāmā, Vyāsa, Kṛpa and Paraśurāma are characters from *Mahābhārata*.

16. Bhīṣma took an oath of remaining unmarried forever for the benefit of his father and because of this he received the boon of →

to the mind, i.e. what would have happened if Bhīṣma had decided to postpone it forever? In the total theistic framework of the text such kind of a question is meaningless. Nonetheless the question remains and also the possibility of interpreting the text in different ways. How does one distinguish between Vyāsa's immortality and Bhīṣma's postponement of death? One level at which the distinction can be made is the birth of these two characters. Vyāsa is born to his parents in a normal or near normal biological process. He was expected to be a human being. On the other hand, Bhīṣma was born to Gaṅgā (river goddess) and he was also not expected to live a human life. He is one of the semi-divine beings called Vasus who were cursed to be born as humans. Gaṅgā became the mother of these cursed Vasus and released them from the human bondage as soon as they were born. Bhīṣma was not so lucky. He lived through the human course of life and on the way acquired the boon of death by choice. Thus, Bhīṣma is a character who represents human bondage and death symbolizes relief. There is no question of Bhīṣma not accepting death. He was to go back through death to his final abode where there is no birth and no death. Time which is perceived through change is meaningless in the case of Bhīṣma. The character of Bhīṣma shows the limitation of sensory perception which is related to human form. The reality of the eternity of time remains beyond it. The illusion of going beyond the process of decay and death with the grossness of total human existence is reflected through this character of Vyāsa.

The ultimate perception of the time can be seen through the character of Kṛṣṇa. Kṛṣṇa of *Mahābhārata* was born like a

---

→ postponing his death till he wishes. The irony is that for a prince, to lose his kingdom to his brothers and not to procreate along with a prolonged life is more of a curse than a boon. (The *Mahābhārata*, Ādiparva).

human being, lived the vibrant life full of activities and died like a common man. He had multiple relations with other human beings which are commonly understood as that of a son, father, brother, husband, friend. And still he was called the "God." There are occasions when he revealed his Godhood. The ultimate revelation is seen in *Bhagavad-Gītā* where he shows his ferocious form.[17] Kṛṣṇa is omnipresent, omnipotent, omniscient, incarnated himself in a human form. His birth was the beginning of his life as an incarnation. He brings himself within the limits of human perception. The shift of his position from omnipotent to a particular form is a part of a larger conceptual framework called *yuga*.[18] It is said that there have been innumerable cycles of these *yuga*s as well as incarnations. The highlight of the concept of *yuga*s is the perception of time as cyclical movement. This has been happening eternally without a beginning or an end. The human experience of time as past, present and future is nothing but an illusion because from the present, past is confirmed and future is anticipated. But the present itself is just a point on the cyclic *yuga* model. *Yuga*s in a way are not the simple reckoning of the datable time but represent the essence of time. Time is emergence, time is sustenance and time is decay and this is in a continuous cycle. Kṛṣṇa of the *Dvāpara yuga*, i.e. Kṛṣṇa of the *Mahābhārata* is a replica of this incomprehensibly huge model. He is born, he acts and he dies. At the same time he is God, hence, he cannot fit into the life frame of the mortals. Is Kṛṣṇa immortal? In the ultimate analysis, this question does not make sense. But at the spatio-temporal level of human beings, with whom he lives, it makes sense and the answer is affirmative.

---

17. *Bhagavad-Gītā*, XI, *viśvarūpa darśana*.

18. Romila Thapar, *Time as a Metaphor of History: Early India* (Delhi: Oxford University Press, 1996), pp. 13–19.

Our problem is of mastering the illusion of time and understanding eternity of time because it is said to be one of the facets of "Reality." Reality is of prime concern. Deep down the levels of human consciousness there is a hope that the life is eternal and the death is not real. This hope is different from the hope of becoming immortal. This hope is the beginning of a pathway towards the understanding of the essence of life.

The *Mahābhārata* by way of the *Gītā* has dealt with this issue in a graphic presentation of *viśvarūpa darśana*. Kṛṣṇa declares, "I am Time, which destroys the world, fully grown, engaged here in destruction of the worlds."[19] Arjuna says in bewilderment, "On seeing your mouths and their terrible tusks like the fires of Time, I do not know the quarters and do not find any comfort."[20]

God is timeless but manifest through time in the scenes of destruction according to the presentation of the ferocious form of the above-mentioned chapter. However it also assumes that the destruction is always a simultaneous element that keeps space with rejuvenation. Thus God proclaims, "I am the eternal Time."[21] God is imperishable, beginningless, unending Time.

To summarize the ultimate perception of time represented in the *Mahābhārata*, one can say that the essence of the whole universal movement is the most evident power of the supreme reality, the God, who is also beginningless and unending and eternal time. This theistic understanding of the Time is the base of the spiritual life in India, distinctly far from the mechanized reckoning of time of the modern world.

---

19. *Bhagavad-Gītā*, XV.32.
20. *Bhagavad-Gītā*, XI.25.
21. *Bhagavad-Gītā*, X.33.

7

Concept of Time in India
A Literary and Philosophical Understanding

H.S. Komalesha & Jaison A. Manjaly

If history is a mode of recollecting and organizing our past or if it is an account of narrating what happened, in terms of an event in time, then it becomes intellectually imperative to interrogate whether there are any other modes of recording our past without any reference to when it exactly happened. With this we face an immediate question — "what is the necessity of invoking the chronology if our aim is to evoke history to influence our present and shape our future?" This interrogation leads our attention towards India, which practised the recording of the past with the least reference to factual representation of time through its creative traditions such as epics, folktales, myths, and other oral and written narratives. But as Ashis Nandy asks, do these modes alternative histories or alternatives to history need to be glossed over in order to construct a different epistemology of the past? In this regard, this article also seeks some relevant answers from Indian philosophy.

Human perception of every event and empirical phenomenon requires two cognitive intersections. To say it differently, an experience becomes an experience only when it gets transcribed by two perceptive markers called space and *time*. If we confine our argument only to time for the obvious practical purpose, we can say that it has always been a ubiquitous human fascination to check, hold, stall, and transgress this ever-flowing time. In order to retrieve the flown time, to put it simply 'the past,' human beings have always attempted to record it; such a recording of time — the always and the already altering dynamic principle — has been done in multiple ways. Behind such endeavours we can trace the human optimism that past, when retrieved and stored, can be a source of guiding principle to shape the present and lead the posterity. And we know that history is one such discipline or can we say a methodology that is brought to serve the purpose? But unfortunately the "historical consciousness" that pervaded during the Enlightenment era has tended to monopolize the past, and this in turn has led to its hegemony over other forms of recording the past. The concept of history itself has become in the words of Ashis Nandy[1] "an imperialism of category" that exhausts the notion of the past. Curiously enough many intellectuals, who we hold in great reverence and admiration, aver that only a few of civilizations or cultures possess the sense of history, and they hold such a sense of historical consciousness as key to intellectual growth, and human progress. None other than a great philosopher such as Hegel, a great thinker like Karl Marx, and an intellectual of the calibre of J.S. Mill join the fray; they opine that cultures, which do not possess the sense of *historical consciousness*, say in this context, Indian cultures, are culturally and civilizationally challenged, a euphemism that we have used to denote their intention that such races are uncultured and uncivilized. Before we examine what they exactly mean by the sense of history, it becomes essential to take a look at

1. Ashis Nandy, "History's Forgotten Doubles", *History and Theory* vol. 34, 2 (1995), pp. 44–66.

what exactly they say about such *uncivilized* cultures.

We can trace this back to one of the earliest written sources and it is related to the work of the peripatetic traveller Alberuni (Muhammad al-Beruni). During his visit to India in about CE 1020, he notes:

> Unfortunately the Hindus do not pay much attention to the historical order of things; they are very careless in relating the chronological succession of their kings, and when they are pressed for information and are at a loss, not knowing what to say, they invariably take to tale-telling.[2]

James Mill, another noted British historian who belongs to a much later generation, too, repeats the comment when he says:

> As soon as reason begins to have considerable influence in the direction of human affairs, no use of letters is deemed more important than that of preserving an accurate record of those events and actions by which the interests of the nation have been promoted or impaired. But the human mind must have a certain degree of culture, before such a memorial is perceived. . . . All rude nations, even those to whom the use of letters has long been familiar, neglect history, and are gratified with the production of the mythologists and the poets. It is allowed on all hands that no historical composition existed in the literature of the Hindus; they had not reached that point of intellectual maturity, at which the value of a record of the past for the guidance of the future begins to be understood.[3]

He views the absence of history among the Hindus as evidence for their cultural inferiority. Even Hegel who was himself not

2. Edward C. Sachau (ed.), *Alberuni's India* (Delhi: S. Chand & Co., 1964), p.11.
3. James Mill, *The History of British India* (London & Chicago: University of Chicago Press, 1975), pp. 198-99.

an Indologist, but relied heavily on Mill's version of India says in his *Lectures on the Philosophy of History* (1831) that Indians lacked the sense of history though they have a treasure in other forms of arts and sciences. While he commends the progress Indians have made when it comes to astronomy, mathematics, algebra, physics, literature, philosophy, and grammar, he laments the lack of History.

> [In India] we find the department of History altogether neglected, or rather non-existent. For History requires understanding — the power of looking at an object in an independent objective light, and comprehending it in its rational connection with other objects. Those peoples therefore are alone capable of History, and of prose generally, who have arrived at that period of development (and can make that their starting point) at which individuals comprehend their own existence as independent, i.e. possesses self-consciousness. . . .
>
> This makes [the Hindoos] incapable of writing History. All that happens is dissipated in their minds into confused dreams. What we call historical truth and veracity — intelligent, thoughtful comprehension of events, and fidelity in representing them — nothing of this sort can be looked for among the Hindoos.[4]

This theme of Indian ahistoricity, viewed *vis-à-vis* the Enlightenment tradition of History is originally invoked in the service of Western imperialism and cultural self-aggrandizement. All these claims and comments are certainly born out of specific and privileged notions of history that are guided by the eighteenth century ideals such as rationality and logical growth. This has made history's claim to past more

---

4. George Wilhelm Friedrich Hegel, *The Philosophy of History* (London: Constable & Co., 1956), pp. 161-62.

scientific accounting for the construction of historiography. But thanks to post-colonial understanding we now are aware of the significance of non-Western notions of time that are equally significant. This understanding has raised certain questions: if *history* is a time-perceptive marker, a mode of recollecting and organizing our past or if it is an account of narrating what happened, in terms of an event in time, then it becomes intellectually imperative to interrogate whether there are any other modes of recording our past without any reference to when it exactly happened. This at once makes us confront a more pertinent question, "what is the necessity of invoking the chronology/time if at all our sole aim is to evoke the past to influence our present and shape the future?" With this interrogation we turn our attention towards India, which prastised the recording of the past with the least reference to factual representation of time. This was done with the help of myths, legends and epics, which defined the cultural past of India. In the Indian post-colonial context history is not a pursuing of chance occurrences nor a sustained concentration and tracing of cause and effects; it is also not a scholarly reporting of facts presented chronologically claiming historiographic authenticity. As Stephen Slemon[5] says in his much acclaimed article, "Post-colonial Allegory and the Transformation of History," in the context of post-colonial cultures history goes beyond the simple binary of either redeeming or annihilating the past. The colonial encounter constricts out notion of history as the "few privileged monuments of achievements," which serves either to arrogate history wholesale to the imperial centre or to erase it from the colonial archive and produce in the Third World cultures

---

5. Stephen Slemon, "Postcolonial Allegory and the Transformation of History", *Journal of Commonwealth Literature*, vol. 23.1 (1988), pp. 157-68.

a condition of what Eddie Baugh[6] calls "historylessness." Both these notions of history are part of imperial myths for both are defined by what is central, and not by what is peripheral. Western notions of History, with capital "H" can be best summarized in the words of Bishop Stubbs: "I will say that the true field of Historic study is the history of those nations and institutions in which the real growth of humanity is to be traced; in which we can follow the developments, the retardations and perturbations, the ebb and flow of human progress, the education of the world."[7] In the Indian post-colonial context there is a very thin line between History and Imperial History because their discursive formation is always mutual. Here, Imperialism, Civilization, White Man's Burden, and other such notions form the essence of History, which in turn resulted in the geographical, socio-cultural aggression of the Empire. Hence from post-colonial perspective history as such becomes an "intolerable pile or a cultural absence," and post-colonial writers attempt through their writing means to go beyond these notions. And hence appropriately our article tries to locate the concept of time as history within the creative traditions of India. Indian epics, folktales, myths, legends and other oral and written narratives serve the purpose of recording the past for a purpose and in a method completely alien to the Western notions. But at this point Ashis Nandy asks, "are these myths alternative histories or alternatives to history?"[8] This needs to be thought over in order to construct a different epistemology of the past. In the Indian context the documentation of the present elapsing into the past was more a matter for creative insurgence rather than a factual

---

6. Edward Baugh, "The West Indian Writer and His Quarrel with History", *Tapia* (27 February 1977), pp. 6-7.
7. Bill Ashcroft, *Postcolonial Transformation* (London: Routledge, 2001).
8. Ashish Nandy (1995), pp. 44-46.

representation. Therefore it was the job of not an historian, and for that matter there was neither one; it was the privileged onus of the creative writer who it was believed is gifted with "vision" not "observation." We can remember Nārada — a divine saint asking Vālmīki to write the story of Rāma after blessing him with *trikāla-jñāna* (vision to see past, present and future). Therefore, in the case of Indian tradition, writing of past invariably entails with it prophesying the future too. For after all the three are triple manifestations of time, and a writer should necessarily be a *seer* too. We are reminded of what W.H. Auden has got to say about poem. For him a poem should be a verbal earthly paradise, a timeless world of pure play, which gives us delight precisely because of its contrast to our historical existence with all its insoluble problems and inescapable suffering.

When we come to Kālidāsa — a much acclaimed Sanskrit poet, we learn he gives us an account of King Bhoja's reign through his *Vikramorvaśīyam* and *Śākuntalam*. While both the works are much historical, where he likens Bhoja to Purāṇic characters such as Purūravā and Duṣyanta, they are also accounts of the problems and perils of people lived during his time. Simultaneously they are the exemplification of the literary and imaginative zeal. This is true of other court poets also. In Kannaḍa literature Pampa — the first great Kannaḍa poet who lived around tenth century CE compares his patron-cum-king Arikeśari to Arjuna (a heroic personality of *Mahābhārata*) writes *Vikramārjuna Vijaya*. The work is again an account of the battles that the king has lost and won; a record of the conditions of the people lived during that time. Ranna, another major Kannaḍa poet who comes a couple of centuries after Pampa, emulates the earlier tradition by writing *Gadāyuddha* where he compares his patron king to Bhīma. Throughout the tradition we learn that writing of the past was no exclusive activity and rather it is tied with the creative traditions. This can be illustrated further by taking a more applicable situation such as Indian Independence movement and a living writer such as Raja Rao. In his novels a whole range of a people's history is sketched out, re-examined, narrativized; there is a creative fusion of fact and fiction, myth and reality. His works demonstrate how even a contemporary political event such as Indian freedom struggle gets transmuted into the mythic traditions of recording the past. Even a very much recent figure of history such as Gandhi becomes a Purāṇic personality. See how he describes Gandhi in his short story *Narsiga*:

> "Who was this Gandhiji?" Narsa had asked. "An old man — a bewitching man, a saint you know! . . . He looks beautiful as morning sun and he wears only a little loincloth like a pariah . . . he is a very great man. They say he is an incarnation of God, and that is why everybody touches his feet, even Brahmins my son. . . ."[9]

In the story the boy sees Gandhi as Rāma and the red-ruler as Rāvaṇa — the monster for whose extermination Viṣṇu had to reincarnate as Rāma. When Gandhi is released from the prison, the whole political event gets a religious notation in the observation of the boy. He likens the event to Rāma's return from exile.

> The Mahatma is going to fly in the air like goddess Sītā and in a flower chariot drawn by 16 steeds . . . they will fly through air and the heavens will let fall a rain of flowers.[10]

His *Kanthapura* too can be cited to illustrate this purpose. The novel records the Gandhian impact on a typical Indian village

---

9. Raja Rao, "Narsiga" in his *The Cow of the Barricades* (London: Oxford University Press, 1947) p. 115.

10. Ibid., p. 119.

through the informal but very intimate narration of an elderly widow Acchakka. Gandhi is again portrayed here as Rāma, Kṛṣṇa, and Śiva. The entire novel speaks volumes for how a creative writer assimilates and transcends a contemporary political reality into the cultural consciousness of a tradition, race and people. This is how recording of past is done for the moral and practical purposes of the future. This is the difference between those who live in history and those who live outside it.

Ashis Nandy brilliantly elaborates this basic difference between societies with history and those without it especially in those societies where myths and legends are the cardinal methods of recording the experiences of the past. He says that all myths are principally morality tales and therefore what is mythical is also essentially moral; in fact we cannot separate the remembered past from its ethical meaning in the present. For this refusal, he categorically asserts, "It is often important not to remember the past, objectively, clearly, or in its entirety." But History cannot take seriously the "principle of forgetfulness." It has to reject the principle as "irrational, retrogressive, unnatural, and fundamentally incompatible with historical sensitivities. Remembering, history assumes, is definitionally superior to forgetting."[11] Upon this distinction we can define history as an organization of the remembered and organized past, and myth as a recollection of that past which has consciously forgotten some details, facts and files. Because for Indians the function of remembering the past is not an exercise in scholarship but a guiding lesson it necessarily involves an element of morality; morality that can be of use to the present and future generations. So what is required for this purpose is not details of what happened to whom, when,

11. Ashis Nandy (1995), pp. 44-46.

and where, but only what happened, because only "what happened" is equally applicable to all of us and nothing else. It was only circumstantial exegesis that made it possible what happened to who it happened and when it happened. Except these accidental values details of whereabouts and whenabouts of the incident are only but secondary.

But for historians the sole purpose is to unravel the past on the basis of a neatly articulated frame of references with complete objectivity. There are neither personal considerations nor expectations out of history. Their whole craftsmanship is nothing more than an intellectual gymnasium meant for scholarly exhibitionism. But again thanks to post-colonial thinking it is commonplace today that there cannot be any objective past. Construction of time is done only through semiotic representation. But while doing so we should be guarded to realize that it is again a filter through which we are viewing time that is no more there. While history is only a mode of perceiving time, there exist several other methods where there is a possibility of plural constructions of time that happen simultaneously. The ecstatic songs and delirious dance in which Mīrā is engaged can take her out of her present time context and make her join several *gopikā*s blissfully dancing around Kṛṣṇa — an event that is ages apart. Devotional empathy that manifests through the writings of Tulsīdāsa can *boot* him out of his time to meet Sītā, Hanumān and Rāma belonging to different *yuga*. Ramakrishna Paramahamsa through his dedicated love could see Jesus, Prophet Mohammed, and Rāma — though all the three belong to different periods. These illustrations amply show that breaking away from the shackles of time and reaching out to that which does not *exist* is in the domains of creativity. If history can only remind us of the bygone time creative arts can virtually and effectively reach the past.

We can also explain the lack of Indian history by taking recourse to some Indian philosophical schools. The lack of historicity and time consciousness in India has its roots in the early philosophical traditions. The six principal schools of philosophy (*ṣaḍ darśana*) as well as Buddhist and Jaina philosophic traditions are also the source of reference to the development of ahistoricity and timelessness in Indian context, which calls for an analysis of Indian metaphysics and epistemology. However the metaphysical interpretations are confronted by certain difficulties that we shall clarify with the epistemological interpretation.

In the metaphysical tradition the state of ultimate liberation — *jīvanmukti* — has always been an icon of the highest human achievement. In order to be liberated one has to get rid of the wheel of *māyā* that operates on the concepts of time and history. In other words time and history bind; *māyā* pins us down to the world, which is ultimately the cause of bondage of the *ātman*. But according to Indian metaphysics, self and consciousness are timeless. They are always and already there — eternally. They are *anādi* and *ananta* like the *Brahman* itself. But the Western notion of history runs counter to these Indian philosophical beliefs wherein what is required is not an invocation of the timelessness, instead a belief in the rootedness in time. Between these beliefs one can almost sense a kind of antithesis that refuses to attain synthesis. J.N. Mohanty's observation comes aptly in this regard:

> What is needed for a sense of history is recognition of the historicity of consciousness. Now, in general, for Hindu thought, consciousness is above change . . . [accepting] a theory of [the temporality of] consciousness would also entail a rejection of that conception of self or *ātman*, which is almost a pervasive feature of Hindu thought. . . . An essential temporality of *ātman* is a necessary presupposition of a

serious philosophical concern for history.[12]

And when we come to Buddhist metaphysics, it seems to pose certain other difficulties to the orthodox understanding of history and time because the very concept of time is being considered there as real. According to the Buddhist conception reality everything is in flux. However the difficulty can be resolved or given an alternative explanation if we examine their concept of *nirvāṇa*. The Buddhist concept of *nirvāṇa*, which appears to be a conceptual translation of the Hindu understanding of *mokṣa*, of course with the minor differences, also emphasizes a journey outside the lodge of time and history. We can offer the philosophical explanations that we have mentioned above and say that even in *nirvāṇa* the necessity of time is only in going beyond it and not in being caught in it by recording it. The attainment of *nirvāṇa* arrests and transcends the momentariness of time and history.

It seems that Indian metaphysics is a weak thesis to uphold the timelessness and ahistoricity at this juncture since there are counter examples, for instance, "How can a person who attains *nirvāṇa* transcend time and history since the rest of his life he remains in this empirical world? However there is another alternative in Indian philosophy to look at this problem from a different point of view. If we locate our problem in the boundaries of epistemology there is a scope of getting rid of the difficulties of the metaphysical interpretation of timelessness and ahistoricity.

In Indian tradition there are various means of acquiring knowledge, such as perception, inference, testimony, etc. However the number of the means of knowledge constructions

12. Jitendra Nath Mohanty, "Between Indology and Indian Philosophy", in *Beyond Orientalism*, ed. Eli Franco and Karin Preisendanz (Amsterdam, 1997), pp. 166-68.

varies from one school to another. Cārvāka school admits only perception and inference as valid means of knowledge. Vaiśeṣika on the other hand is sceptical about the validity of testimony. In spite of these differences among the various schools of philosophy "memory" (*smṛti*) is not considered as valid source of knowledge by any of the schools. "Memory," according to them, is not compatible with the genuine knowledge, which is defined in terms of novelty, correspondence and independence. It is obvious that memory lacks novelty since it is only a recollection of the past. It also does not correspond with the object of knowledge because the object of "memory" no longer exists. Again, it also lacks independence because "memory" cannot invoke its object without any reference to the past. In the backdrop of this understanding of memory, which is central to the Western notion of history, we have enough reasons to know why time and history have been neglected in Indian tradition. Such a history, according to Indian philosophical schools, adds nothing new to the existing volume of knowledge, therefore it does not enjoy their serious attention.

In the same way "testimony" which is a valid means of knowledge also rejects the authenticity of secular history as genuine because it falls out of the authority of Vedas. In other words a "testimony" is not a genuine means of knowledge unless it is derived from the authority of Vedas, which is considered to be authorless and timeless. Given these reasons we are now in a position to appreciate why history and time were incompatible with the metaphysical and epistemological tradition of Indian philosophy.

With this we arrive at a point where we realize that time — the kinetic principle of the cosmos as manifested through *history* — becomes a confining factor for the achievements of bigger human goals. Except its mythical component, which incidentally is also a moral component, there is no scholarly significance attached to the notion of history; hence the literary smearing to the recording of the past. However all these references of the concept of time and history to Indian philosophy and its creative traditions, we are aware, raise more problematizing issues and explore more questions rather than giving satisfactory answers, and we know that right questions are more important because they set human exploration always on the alert.

8

Time in North Indian Music[1]

Sushil Kumar Saxena

THE purpose of this brief article is twofold: first, to determine the role of time (as rhythm) in Hindustānī (or north Indian) music;[2] and, second, to discuss whether the (semblance of) time that we see here is similar to or different from time as we experience it in daily life.

To speak quite generally, music builds upon time in two distinctive ways, as rhythm and as aesthetic pace. By the pace that I purposely call aesthetic I mean not only the tempo at which music flows over different notes, but the time taken in singing or playing a single note, that is, the duration of abidance at individual notes. In both these forms, and in accordance with the varying demands of ongoing music, aesthetic pace may be regulated (as in *ālāpa* of *dhruvapada*-singer)[3] entirely by the musician's own aesthetic sense, and

1. Material for a part of this essay is provided by my article: "Hindustani Rhythm and An Aesthetical Issue" which appeared in *Sangeet Natak*, offical journal of Sangeet Natak Akademi, New Delhi, nos. 129-30, 1998, pp. 34-37.
2. I may add that a good deal of what I have said in this essay is true of south Indian rhythm as well.
3. *Ālāpa* is singing without words and also without the aid of (beat-measured) rhythm. *Dhruvapada* which follows is song which employs both words and rhythm. A *rāga* (or melody-type) is common to both *ālāpa* and *dhruvapada*.

quite without the aid of beats — which is why I call it aesthetic pace. By rhythm, on the other hand, I only mean that pace which is measured with the help of beats. In the way we generally talk about Hindustani music, aesthetic pace is *laya*, and rhythm is *tāla*.

But, one may here wonder, what exactly is the warrant for relating rhythm with time? My ready answer is: the fact that the two share some features visibly. Time flows, so does music. We generally measure the flow of time in real life by marking the ticks of a clock; and the flow of rhythm in music by noticing the succession of beats. As a rule, ticks and beats are alike articulate. Succession or the before-after order is another feature which time and music share. This is specially true of Indian music which eschews the use of two different notes at the same point of time except in the case of, say, a *jugalabandī*[4] by two different instrumentalists where the playing of a *vādi* (or focal) note by one may at once be supplemented with the marking of a *saṁvādi* (or consonant) note by the other. Further, the cyclic and repetitive quality that distinguishes clock-time is a feature of Hindustānī music as well — I mean, of its rhythmic aspect in particular. The bulk of our music is "accompanied" by the repetitive playing of a *ṭhekā* (or the anchor of a rhythm) which is plainly cyclic in character, for it begins from, and returns to the first beat, making this beat appear as the focal one (*sama*). Clock time is however quite different from time as we experience (not measure) it in daily life. The content of clock time is provided by ticks and the moving hands. What fills our "lived" time is, on the other hand, experience — of both doing and suffering. The span of a clocked hour does not change unless some defect creeps into the timing device. In real life, on the other hand,

4. By *jugalabandī* I here mean a duet of instrumental music.

what is literally a one-hour waiting for a loved one may feel like an eternity. But is this experienced time not so dissimilar to musical time or rhythm? This is the question which I may now address, primarily because it is being debated in contemporary aesthetics. However, before I actually begin doing so it seems necessary to see what rhythm in our music really is.

The essential purpose of Hindustānī rhythm (as an independent art)[5] is to establish a basic cycle of steadfast pace, and to create patterns of infinite variety within its bounds, both with the help of beats and *bolas*[6] (or mnemonic syllables) which not only christen the beats (so to say), but provide a decorative filling between and across them, yet never in such a way that the regulative and formative character of the focal beat (of the cycle) may be wantonly disregarded, they (or the syllables) themselves — and so also the patterns which they go to make — being quite capable of being memorized and winsomely recited.

Let me now bring out the key ideas implicit in this summary characterization of rhythm:

a. To begin with, we may note that the matrix of all trellis-work in Hindustānī rhythm is a cycle. It

5. For the view that rhythm may well be regarded as an independent art, see my essay, "Aesthetic Theory and Hindustani Rhythm" in *The British Journal of Aesthetics*, Summer 1976, vol. 16, no. 3, reprinted in my book, *The Winged Form — Aesthetical Essays on Hindustani Rhythm* (New Delhi: Sangeet Natak Akademi, 1979), pp. 1-17.

6. What the Indian (classical) drummer plays is not mere beats, but *bols* which are tied to, and spread over beats. So an ensemble which presents both Western and Indian drums is not really conducive to a proper appreciation of Indian rhythm; for it generally highlights only the parity of beats in respect of number and disposition.

comprises a specific number of beats. But these beats are not alone here. Tied to everyone of them, and often spread over them, there is a letter or a bunch of letters[7] — such as *kā, dhit, tirkit, dhā, ā* — which are all without verbal meanings, and which only resemble, more or less, the sounds of the beats (as played). It is this linkage of beats with specific letters which makes it easy for us to recognize and remember the different sounds which the playing of the cycle (and the patterns) produces. Even the off beat, which is not actually sounded on the drum, but only gently hinted at or visualized, carries a syllable as its indicator.

b. It is important to see how exactly the matrix of Hindustani rhythm is cyclic, and how this character determines all creation in the region of this art. In following the rhythm which the matrix in question embodies and projects we not only set out from the first beat, but return to it, completing a round, so to say, and (I repeat) making the first beat appear focal. This beat is, indeed, of special value here. The cycle, and the patterns that may be woven across it — and ultimately within it — have all to attain to the focal beat (called *sama*) with split-second accuracy.[8] This is something which the drummer has to bear in mind all along, as a basic requirement. Further, the *sama* is the beat where the cycle and the patterns all attain to completion of their individual forms.

c. Above all, a pattern owes its excellence as such also to the general shapeliness of the way in which it realizes

7. Mere letters, I repeat, not (meaningful) words.

8. Corresponding to what is called *āmada* in Hindustānī music, meaning a segment which strikes the discerning listener as an orderly approach to the focal beat.

the *sama*. Every pattern is a configuration, an organized whole. In some cases, however, it is distinguished by a specific terminal segment where, because of its orientation, the pattern appears to gather its beauty, and to proceed to deliver it at the *sama*. Yet the *sama* is not only the target of patterns, but their apex where they themselves appear to flower.[9] This suggestion of (what may be called) efflorescence is irresistible where the pattern's overall shapeliness is capped with such a playing of the same beat that the sound produced may seem to accomplish itself instantly. The beauty here arises, so to say, from an electric chipping of the *sama*-instant (or stroke) itself. No other art, I believe, provides a better instance of the aesthetic divisibility of minimal time, or of the power of a mere point to lend both beauty and wholeness to what paves the way to it.

d. A very interesting feature of *bola*s is their audile character. It is (the *bola*) so rich in variety that it can easily hold discriminating attention for long. Some *bola*s, indeed appear to sparkle like a star, and others engage the ear with their wedge-like alacrity in saving two adjacent syllables from collision, so to say. Coupled with due accentuation of some syllables and regulated variation of the pace of the segments that they generally go to make, this fascinating diversity of their character as sheer sounds makes Indian rhythm[10] a quite uncommon object of aesthetic contemplation. Its content is neither meaningful speech nor a mere medley of indistinct sounds, such as may

9. The Hindi/Urdu word, here, is *khilanā*, meaning "to blossom.

10. Not merely north Indian rhythm.

be produced by the jostling of utensils in a big bag, but series of differently ordered, but all identifiable alphabets of our native languages. Form is perhaps more manifestly articulate in Indian rhythm that in the other arts.[11]

e. Further, what shapes the essential features of form — that is, the run and inner knitting of patterns — is a necessary orientation. As a rule, patterns have to terminate in a clear and articulate show of the *sama*. Further, it is desirable that before they actually hit the target, so to say, they may appear to be making for it. The critic judges their quality (as patterns) largely by checking if these two requirements are met. Conjointly, they make a very clear criterion indeed. But, I hasten to add, some patterns — that is, those which represent the *atīta* and *anāgata* kinds — are so designed that they end expressly — and therefore, not wantonly — a little after or before the focal beat. In such cases, the beat in question is, of course, not played; but insofar as the drummer's adroit avoidance of it is intentional, it is duly kept in mind, if quietly. Such "giddy cunning,"[12] in fact only heightens our awareness of the form[13] of

---

11. Clear, however, only to those who can follow the extent and distinctive idiom of the cycle.
12. I have here in mind Milton's reference to the "wanton heed and giddy cunning" of good music.
13. Cf.: "Form does not lie simply in the correct observance of rules. It lies in the struggle of certain living material to achieve itself within a pattern. The very refusal of a poet to sacrifice what he means to a perfectly correct rhyme, for example, can more powerfully suggest the rhyme than correctness itself would". Stephen Spender: *World within World* (London: Hamilton, 1951) pp. 313-14.

> both the cycle and the pattern,[14] assuming of course that we are able to follow, in due accordance, the course of the pattern — which can sometimes be pretty intricate — without losing our hold on the basic pace as embodied in the cycle.[15]

The onward flow of the pattern, brisk or leisurely, is of course not the same thing as the felt passage of life as lived; quite unlike the latter, the former is a decorative run directed towards a mere moment — the moment of the focal beat. Yet, the sense of time (or a semblance of it) may be said to be there not only in our everyday experience, but in our contemplation of rhythm. But are the two appearances of time essentially similar?

We cannot at once say no. Patterns in rhythm are not only serial, but concurrent. They comprise beats (and *bola*s) that we see running as a series. But successiveness, or the before-after order, is not the only feature of lived time that the art of rhythm builds upon. Simultaneousness is another. As a rule, we have seen, the terminal syllable of a pattern is also the moment of perfect coincidence with the *sama*-instant. Further, when it has been perfectly established, the cycle appears to endure as a stable frame in relation to which the quality of patterns is largely discerned. But if the formal features of time as ordinarily experienced all serve as the material of time as it appears in rhythm, is there no essential difference between the two?

Aestheticians are divided on this issue. Thus, whereas

---

14. Because of this dual engagement of attention, contemplation of patterns in rhythm may be said to be bifocal, in a way.

15. After a few rounds of proper playing, a cycle comes to look firmly set or unwavering. "Establish" is the right word for what is called *qāyem karanā* in Urdu.

Langer,[16] M. Sauvage,[17] and Basil de Selincourt[18] take pains to distinguish time in music (or rhythm)[19] as "virtual" and "special," or as an "ideal substitute" of ordinary time, Philip Alperson[20] sees no essential difference between the two. He admits that music gives rise to a specific class of tensions. But, he continues, what is there to prevent us from saying that the build-up and release of musical tensions is experienced in the same way as the rise and ebb of life-tensions, that is, in a before-after order? And if the two kinds of tensions are experienced in the same way, how is it warranted to say that music creates an order of virtual time? Generally, it is as an important element of music that rhythm makes its presence and power felt; and insofar as the same "mental functions of attention, memory, and expectation which are characteristic of music perception seem to apply to the perception of noise" too in daily life, it seems improper to hold that the experience of the temporality of specifically musical phenomena . . . [is] *sui generis*.[21]

This argument, however, is not likely to convince one who takes rhythm as it is freely regarded in India, that is, as an

---

16. S.K. Langer, *Feeling and Form* (New York: Routledge and Kegan Paul, New York, Third Impression 1963) pp. 109-10.
17. M. Sauvage's essay "Notes on the Superposition of the Temporal Modes in Works of Art", in *Reflections on Art*, ed. S.K. Langer (Baltimore: The John Hopkins Press, Baltimore, 2nd printing 1960) p. 162.
18. Basil D. Selincourt's "Music and Duration," *Reflections on Art*, ed. Susan Langer (Baltimore: John Hopkins Press, 1958) p. 153.
19. Not as an autonomous art.
20. Philip Alperson's essay " 'Musical Time' and Music as an 'Art of Time' ", in *The Journal of Aesthics and Art Criticism* (Summer 1980) p. 441.
21. Ibid., p. 412.

autonomous art too, with its own unique material, creative devices and criterion of evaluation. And he could put his dissent quite simply, say as follows:

Suppose two essentially dissimilar orders of time are really there. Where could the difference lie? Not in the (alleged) absence, in one of them, of the formal features we have distinguished, like continuance and successiveness; for without these features, time would be a mere word. Nor could we say that one of them is quite without content. Such a time too would be a sheer abstraction. Even our moments of vacancy have a filling of some discontent or ennui. Therefore, the difference we are seeking could only lie in the specific character — and some inner arrangements — of the content of the two temporal orders. But if this conclusion is accepted — and I do not see how it can be refuted — the time that we find in rhythm must be said to be quite different from the temporality that makes the fabric of our daily living; for, whereas the content of the former is provided (we have seen) by beats, *bolas*, and varying pace, that of lived time comprises sequences of events in the outer world — which a person may only notice detachedly — and his own doing and suffering. As for the argument that the two temporal orders, rhythmic and everyday, cannot be regarded as being quite dissimilar because the same mental acts or attitudes are involved in our experiencing them, it is, in my view, quite unavailing. Would it make sense to deny the distinctness of sweet from salted food on the ground that they are both known by tasting? It is, I repeat, not how we experience them, but what exactly we experience in them that makes the two orders of time quite different from each other.

Indeed, the time that we experience as rhythm forms a world of its own, with features that are not to be found anywhere else. A *tablā* maestro dwells in the world of rhythm

— comprising beats, *bola*s, and regular patterns — with as perfect a sense of encompassment as a scientist in that of symbols and formulae. And "happenings" in the drummer's words can be quite out of the ordinary. Where, for instance, in the everyday world do we create beauty, as we may easily do in the rhythm, by deviating (for a while) designedly from a set course, with meaningless letters alone as our material of creation? Even generally, the time that we regulate and beautify purposely cannot be the same as the time which is only given to us and is so often the focus of unforeseen events.

9

Time: A Presentation

Bimalaprasad Mohapatra

THIS combination of words and visuals is an artist's way of reacting to questions about the relationship between creation and time. Creation begins from chaos and at its highest point dissolves into flux. It is only in time that creation takes place — a very vital point for any artist or creator who finds himself or herself immersed in time — and yet, any creation at its supreme point transcends time understood in the sense of temporality. These are some of the points which have been made through the interweaving of words and images presented below. The editors have not in any way tried to disturb or modify the interrelation of words and images thus presented.

— Editors

From fervour kindled to its height
Eternal Law and Truth were born:
Thence was the night produced,
and thence the billowy flood of sea arose.
From that same billowy flood of sea
the year was afterwards produced,
Ordainer of the days nights,
Lord over all who close the eye.
Dhatar, the great creator, then formed
in due order sun and moon.
He formed in order heaven and earth,
the regions of the air, and light.

— *Ṛgveda* 10.190[1]

1. *Hymns of the Ṛgveda*, tr. R.T.H. Griffith (Delhi: Motilal Banarsidass, 4th edn., 2004).

This is how time is related to creation, with the latter a corollary of the former and arising out of it. The creation (*sṛṣṭi*) begins with *Oṁ* or *Amen* or *Alif-lam-mim* or *Aa-U-Ma* — a point of time in the subconscious. As *Māṇḍūkya Upaniṣad* connotes: it is the past, the present, the future. It is the waking state that transcends bounds of human endurance. The Void that perpetually persists between the point of stagnation and growth-potential is the time — time eternal.

A conscious perception of time in measurable terms has been made possible through the cosmic configuration of space and energy. The verifiable units of time like day, night, a month, a season, a year, etc. all form a part of a process of linear progression in the act of creation.

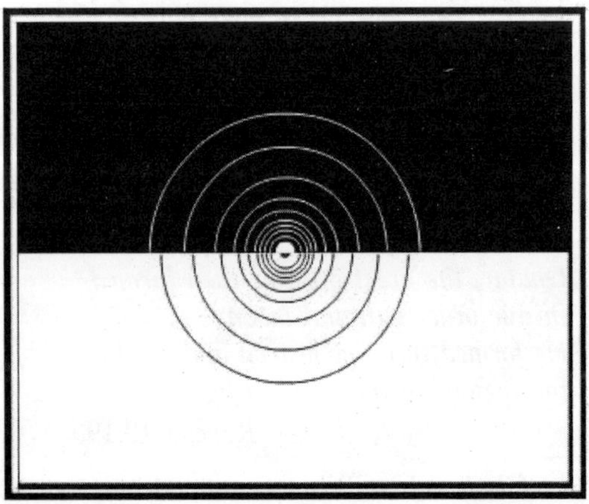

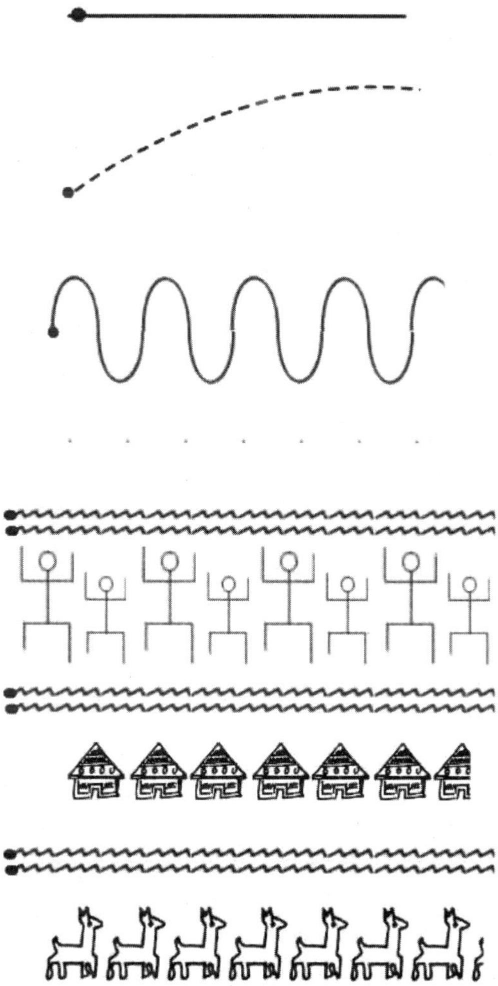

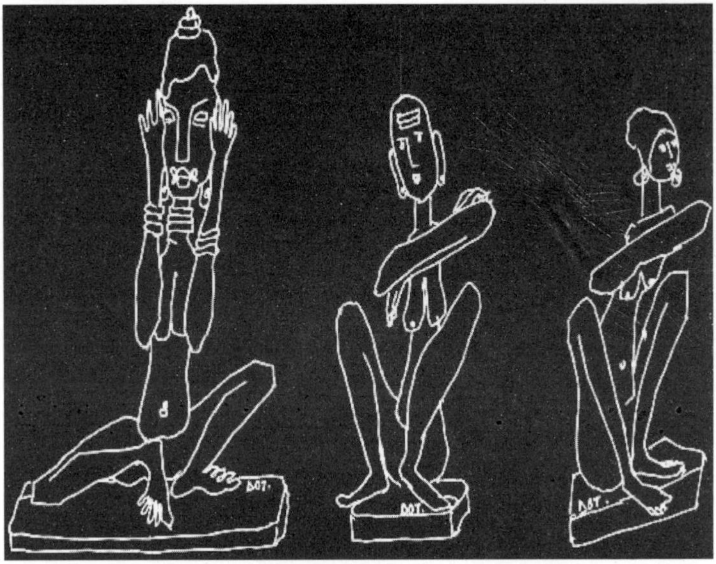

This is how things grow.

This process of progression of time along the lines of growth-potential extends the point of stagnation to line-segments, arcs and curves, and the frequency distribution in this process of progression of time further manifests them into innumerable inanimate patterns. In turn it assimilates these inanimate patterns into nature (*prakṛti*). Forms and modes (*guṇas*) born of *prakṛti* (*Gītā*, 13.19). The inanimate patterns animate into forms. Consciousness/motion is instilled in them. The point of stagnation turns into life-force with its endless manifestations.

Time influences modes through virtuous and vicious cycle of progression. The virtuous cycle of progression creates aesthetic synergy that tends to perfect the creation. Dawn, dusk, summer, winter or autumn, they all blend their dynamics of dimension and colour with modes. The intensity of modes (*guṇas*) — *sattva, rajas* and *tamas* with reference to time either in individual context or in collective and social context, and their resultant reinforcement attributes to categorization and segregation of creation. Positive reinforcement leads to perfection. Here the point of stagnation blossoms into a real being. The sense of realization of the artist/creator inculcates eternal value. In the process of progression of time, colour and dimension — dynamics result in spatial enforcement on the planes of a canvas and carve out visual depth, that propels vision into the horizons, where colours speak louder than the voice.

And when dimension-dynamics start acting upon any mass time turns them all into something bolder than any living objects and elevates the visible to subtle — a state of ecstasy.

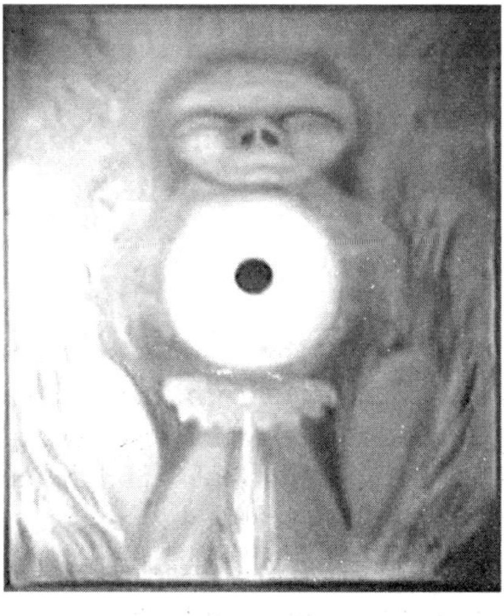

The virtuous cycle of progression of time transcends the creation into a state of super consciousness, where creation does not stick to forms — it becomes multidimensional. It is the stage of fusion where time is lost in the bellow of a sea of time. Forms ultimately lead to formlessness and only a consciousness prevails in the subconscious. It relates: Time past and time future . . . where past and future are gathered . . . pointing to one end . . . which is always present.[2]

2. T.S. Eliot, *The Four Quarters, Collected Poems*, 1909-1962 (New York: Harcourt Brace Jovanovich, 1992).

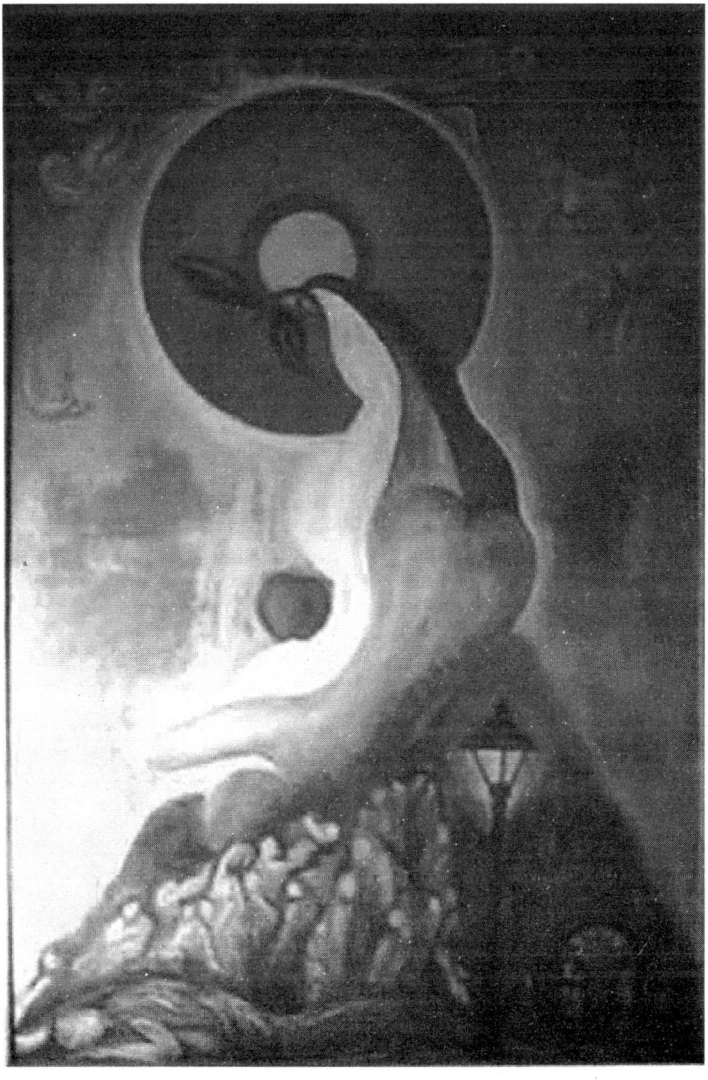

10

Time and the Rāgamālā Tradition

A Brief Exploration

Priyadarshi Patnaik

TIME can perhaps only be experienced when concretized. Young leaves bud, grow, turn deep green, then yellow and fall off and dry to a crackle. We say, "Time has passed." Poets write about this passage of time, without anywhere ever talking about time — they talk about the change of seasons, the transformation of day into night or night into day. Painters paint this passage of time in a sequence as in Buddhist *Ṭaṅkā* paintings depicting the life and *parinirvāṇa* of the Buddha in a series of linked images in a space that is both continuous and yet separated by different backgrounds depicting different contexts for one familiar with the stories. In Pahāṛī paintings one sees depiction of the whole story on a single cloth or paper — the sequence of Rādhā searching for Kr̥ṣṇa and finally getting united with him in the same space separated in a stylized way by leaves or boughs of the forest. In such cases we have a number of images of the Buddha or of Rādhā and Kr̥ṣṇa in the same painting. This is essentially exploring the "change" dimension of things in time through art forms.

The other approach to time is rather contradictory to the very nature of time itself. A moment in time is "frozen" in order to attempt to understand the very nature of that moment. An effort to understand time is made through an act of dissection — a kind of cross-section study. Since time cannot be grasped, is invisible and only leaves its marks, these marks are taken up. One is no longer trying to depict change but the quintessence of a specific moment. Interestingly, this involves a presupposition that time or certain contexts generated by time are cyclic.[1] Unless one assumes so, how can the fundamental markers of time caught and codified in the art forms be recognized again a second time! Instead of time if we speak of temporal experience, the assumption is that temporal experiences are not merely linear. Else, they can neither be contemplated and communicated, nor recognized by others. Spring can only be experienced because it comes again and again; so also with different times of the day or night. Not only that, the day and night have different qualities at different times that leave their impressions on human consciousness. These are depicted. More important, time, whatever it be, affects, influences, pervades living and it is this which is experienced, recognized, and an attempt is made to catch it.

Time-awareness is a part of most reflective traditions. Abstraction of time as *kāla* in the Indian reflective tradition is discussed at some length in the Vaiśeṣika school, in grammar, in Buddhism. However, when one looks at the art tradition of India, concretisation rather than contemplation of *kāla* is reflected. Time is not so much symbolized as personified. Nowhere does one find the depiction of *kāla* or *samaya*. In the *Dharma* tradition Naṭarāja is a case in point. Here is a dancer who dances creation in and out of cosmic existence and

---

1. Cycles form an essential aspect of Hindu, Jaina and Buddhist traditions. Rebirth presupposes cycles or periodicity and this pervades both our philosophies and cultures.

presupposes the cyclic nature of existence.[2] Yama symbolically represents another effect of time — the end of a particular state of being.[3]

In Indian culture stories are often transformed into sculptures and art. Fine arts and plastic arts emerge out of stories, to house stories in temples around gods. Thus, we have the frescoes of Ajantā and the sculptural panels of Khajurāho. Similarly, words are framed to songs and are sung. But they are sung in the context of the generation of "appropriateness." Appropriateness is a very significant concept in Indian culture, especially temporal appropriateness conceptualized as *kṣaṇa* or *muhūrtta*. There is an appropriate time for birth and there is an auspicious time for death. That which is inappropriate is inauspicious. In the dramatic tradition, appropriate time of the day and year are specified for the different types of performances.[4]

It is equally true for music. A *rāga* must be sung in its appropriate time.[5] *Hiṇḍolā* is for spring; *Megha* is for the rainy season; *Dīpaka* is for summer. Walter Kaufmann writes:

---

2. "The dance, in fact, represents His five activites (*pañcakṛtya*), viz. *sṛṣṭi* (overlooking, creation, evolution), *sthiti* (preservation, support), *saṁhāra* (destruction, evolution), *tirobhava* (veiling, embodiment, illusion, and also, giving rest), *anugraha* (release, salvation, grace)." Ananda Coomaraswamy, *The Dance of Shiva* (New York: Sun Wise Turn, 1918), p. 58.

3. Yama figures significantly both in the Upaniṣads (*Kaṭha*) and the Purāṇas.

4. Plays were not supposed to be performed at noon, at midnight or during the time of evening prayer. In this sense there was a lot of freedom. Manmohan Ghosh, *Nāṭyaśāstra* (Calcutta: Royal Asiatic Society, 1950), p. lvi.

5. Swami Prajnanananda, *A History of Indian Music* (Kolkata, Ramakrishna Vedanta Matha, 1963).

> Someśvara seems to be the first Sanskrit author who associates six of his *rāgas* with the Indian seasons: *Śrī-rāga* is to be performed in winter, *Vasanta* (as the name indicates) in spring, *Bhairava* in summer, *Pañcama* in fall, *Megha* in the rainy season and *Naṭanārāyaṇa* in the early winter. Indian music of the present time also uses among its hundreds of *rāgas*, the famous names of Someśvara's six seasonal *rāgas*.[6]

Interestingly, music also has a magic quality of engenderment. Even when sung out of season and time, it can evoke the appropriate time and thus create the appropriate context and ambience. The story of Tansen of Akbar's court is a case in point.[7] And this context and ambience, since they are emotion-dependent, are linked to certain times of days, or the year which conventionally generate them. In other words, time pervades the art tradition, but unconsciously, and visualized in its effects and manifestations. This is especially true of the Indian art tradition.

Some of the points made above need to be clarified and then demonstrated. The rest of the article attempts to do so with the help of the Rāgamālā art tradition.

While *kāla* is a significant philosophical concept, in the Indian literary or fine arts tradition, it is "invisible." In other words, it is present, pervasive and yet never directly discussed. *Bhāgavata Purāṇa* discusses the divisions of time

---

6. Walter Kaufmann, "*Rasa, Rāga-Mālā* and Performance Times in North Indian *Rāgas*", *Ethnomusicology*, vol. 9, no. 3 (September 1965), pp. 272-91.

7. Singing *rāga Dīpaka* set off such powerful vibrations that it almost rained fire and Tansen could have lost his life. By prior arrangement, his disciple sang *Megha Malhāra* to bring rain and revive him — so the legend goes.

and compares time spans of different *loka*s. It also talks of cycles.[8] Yama in *Kaṭha Upaniṣad* personifies the effect of time on human beings — Death. But time is perhaps not "problematized," not even in the Indian philosophical tradition; probably because life is cyclic and it will all happen again. In other words, the passage of time is not an issue, nor is it a problem or matter of great concern. But things happen in time, are affected by specific moments of time and this pervades literary and art traditions. Auspicious and inauspicious moments pervade Indian literature and find place in Indian art. In the Hindu aesthetic tradition *rasa* or aesthetic relish is possible only through a process of perception, of cause and effect, of manifestation of outward signs in actors or characters of effects of what happened before that. Spring affects the love-ravished lover and this love is manifested in spring through its scents and blossoms. Signs of certain specific times (say spring) are internalized and signs of certain emotions or mental states (say love or quickness of heart) are manifested at the appropriate time (for instance spring) and later come to be associated with it. *Śṛṅgāra* (erotic *rasa*) is a case in point.[9]

Thus, while the passage of time may not be the central point of focus, timeliness or specific points of time (*muhūrtta*) are very significant markers in the Indian tradition. This aspect of time virtually has no place in Indian reflective or *darśana*

8. "Time, which in itself is undifferentiated and has no beginning or end, appears in the form of metamorphosis of worldly phenomena. . . . As the universe exists today, so it was before and so it will continue to be hereafter." *Śrīmad Bhāgavata Mahāpurāṇa* (III, 11-13), tr. C.L. Goswami (Gorakhpur: Gita Press, 1971).

9. "It arises from (*uddīpana*) *vibhāva*s such as (a representation of) seasons, garlands, . . ." (*Nāṭyaśāstra*, VI.45). See J.L. Masson and M.V. Patwardhan, *Aesthetic Rapture*, vol. I (Poona: Bhandarkar Oriental Research Institute, 1970), p. 49.

tradition, but it pervades its culture and in the process its art tradition as well. If an analogy can be used, time is like a mighty snake looping languidly and holding on to its own tail. As we pass by we must note the marks on its body because when exactly we do what, having reached which part of its body, looking at which map of textures on its skin, is very significant and will affect our lives. At what time are we born, at what point are we initiated into *brahmacarya*, when exactly do we marry, make love, do other important things in life are very significant. Time passes. There is nothing to say about it. It is nothing to think about. But what exactly do we do at different points of the different loops of the visible markers of time — cycles of day and night, cycles of seasons, cycles of lives, and cycles of moon, planets and stars as they move near and away from the earth — is very vital. They influence our states of mind, our emotions and the paths that our lives take. There are good markers (*śubha muhūrtta*) and bad markers (*aśubha muhūrtta*) of loops of time. Muhūrttaśāstra (Jyotiṣa or astrology) researches it, *nīti* and Dharmaśāstras (dealing with codes of conduct) codify it and the various other knowledge systems used in everyday life make use of it.

Thus, there is an auspicious time for starting a religious painting, sculpture or architectural work, and it is possible to depict this auspicious time in a painting as well. *Rāga*s are delegated their appropriate times as well, probably on the basis of the psycho-physiological moods apt for times of days or years. *Nāṭya* or performance has its apt time (as discussed earlier) as well and so also has dance.

This is the point — time is all pervasive in the Indian literary and art tradition and yet invisible. What we have instead are various points in day or night, seasons and what animals, plants and human beings do or ought to do at those points. We also have the consequence or possible consequence of those actions. Thus, what philosophers debate about — time's non-graspability and yet palpability — is reflected in such traditions.

It is in the background of such an understanding of time in the Indian context that an attempt is being made here to look at the Rāgamālā music and painting.

Let us now briefly discuss this tradition. Rāgamālās (or garland of *rāga*s) are compositions which are to be sung one after the other without break. As with a garland, or a rosary, when one comes a full circle one can start with the first *rāga* again. It is expected to symbolically coincide with the cycle of seasons. Thus, there is a correspondence between time (meaning a specific point in time and its effect on nature and human beings) and the specific *rāga* to be sung at that point. The Rāgamālā, thus, symbolically represents the cycle of seasons, the completion of a year. In due course, this music tradition got linked to certain meditative traditions. The links were the deities with whom the *rāga*s were generally associated. For *rāga Bhairava,* as the name suggests, the associated deity is Bhairava or Śiva. In certain meditative traditions, one is expected to meditate on a deity of one's choice visualizing as clearly as possible this deity in full clarity in one's mind. The musician was supposed to meditate on the image of the deities until they almost became an embodied reality — a physically manifest essence that was the musician's goal through his or her music. In order to aid meditators *dhyāna-śloka*s (short verses to aid meditation) were available which depicted that specific deity in all his/her iconographic detail. In the Indian music tradition, right from the time of *Rāgasāgara* (approximately second century CE)[10] *dhyāna*s are to

10. Kaufmann, p. 280; also found in other important treatises like Sāraṅgadeva's *Saṅgīta Ratnākara, dhyāna-śloka*s, *Rāgataraṅgiṇī* of Locana Kavi, to name a few.

be found associated with specific *rāgas*. Thus, here we find the personification of a *rāga* with attributes as well as ambience spelt out. The *rāga* which may internalize, say, spring, through the *śloka,* manifests spring visually in the form of a personification as well as associated ambience — trees in blossom, etc. From this point it is but one step to paint these deities and we have Rāgamālā paintings. It is thus that we have a threefold attempt to catch different aspects of time (both seasons and times of day) through music, verse and painting.[11] Kaufmann gives an example of *dhyāna-śloka* in *Rāgasāgara* (where it was perhaps used to induce or evoke the *rāga* in the musician's mind) and in a sixteenth century work (*Rāgamālā* of Meṣakarṇa, 1509) where it was perhaps used to either inspire or show the inspiration that induced the painter to paint:

> The sea of notes and microtones, with nectar of all varieties of rhythms and time-measures, the fulfilments of the desire of the worship of Śiva, with the body always besmeared with ashes, decked with matted locks, with the shine of the young moon on the head, with skulls as decorations, I adore Bhairava, the skilful dancer.
>
> — *Dhyāna* on *rāga Bhairava* in *Rāga-sāgara*[12]

And

> Of white complexion, dressed in white garments, carrying the half-moon, the horn and garland, thus appears

---

11. ". . . a mood is given expression through three separate media," writes Reis Flora. However, the link of this mood to time is not mentioned. "Miniature Paintings: Important Sources for Musical History", in *Performing Arts in India: Essays on Music, Dance, and Drama* by Bonnie C. Wade, Betty True Jones, Judy Van Zile, Jon B. Higgins, Regula Burckhardt Qureshi, Naomi Owens, Reis Flora, Source: *Asian Music,* vol. 18, no. 2 (Spring–Summer, 1987), p. 196.

12. Kaufmann, op. cit., p. 281.

> Bhairava, originating from the mouth of Śiva. Around his neck he carries the poison and his eyes are reddened. In his hands he holds the trident, the skull and the lotus blossom. He is adorned with jewels in his ears and his hair. Bhairava is propitiated by the gods on autumn mornings.
>
> — *Dhyāna* on *rāga Bhairava* in *Rāgamālā*[13]

Now, if in *Rāgasāgara dhyāna*s induced the musical mood, what function could the Rāgamālā *dhyāna*s and paintings probably perform? Klaus Ebeling, in his book on Rāgamālā paintings says,

> These garlands of *rāga*s were devices of memorization and classification for the musician who associated the individual modes with deities to whom the *rāga*s were dedicated. Poets then became intrigued with this deification of *rāga*s and spun elaborate situations around their characters. In fact, the poetic versions conjure up images that often have a more human than divine quality or combine both in a fashion typical of many religious concepts in India.[14]

But perhaps, the process of Rāgamālā paintings is much more organic, much deeply rooted in the way people in a particular socio-cultural context navigate in time, experience time and manifest emotions to such experiences, than Ebeling suggests. Nor are they mere "non-musical representation of musical modes" as Charles Capwell points out.[15] For one thing, as Kaufmann points out, *dhyāna*s were used to describe *rāga*s more than a thousand years before the Rāgamālā paintings:

> Beginning with the *Rāgasāgara,* a work often ascribed to Nārada (even to Dattila, second century), we find in addition to lists of *rāga*s short *dhyāna*s, *rāga* descriptions in poetic

13. Kaufmann, op. cit., p. 281.
14. Klaus Ebeling, *Rāgamālā Painting* (New Delhi: Ravi Kumar, 1973) p. 14.
15. Charles Capwell, "A Rāgamālā for the Empress", *Ethnomusicology*, vol. 46, no. 2 (Spring-Summer 2002) p. 198.

> form which, centuries later, led to the pictorial representation of the *rāgas*.
>
> With the invasions of the Mohammedans in the twelfth-century north Indian music underwent considerable changes. New *rāgas* were created by combining Islamic and Indian elements, new musical forms such as the *khayāla* came into existence and musicians and theorists paid greater attention to the fascinating new musical details than to matters of *rasa* and performance time.[16]

It is important to note, secondly, that Rāgamālā paintings emerge during the time of Muslim regime in India, a period of cultural ferment which impacted both music and miniature painting. Perhaps a specific accident of creative imagination was required, and it took a thousand years for that to happen (perhaps at the "appropriate" time).

Rāgamālā paintings, thus, can be said to internalize in them a number of traditions — namely that of music, of storytelling, of the amalgam of the religious and secular, and of meditation. It implies that the *dhyāna-ślokas* are made manifest by the competent artist.[17] Informally, it internalizes a number of Indian traditions. For instance, it internalizes the *rasa* tradition with its emphasis on suggestion. In the hands of the master, and in the eye of the connoisseur, suggestions (like a specific flower, bird or tree, the colour of the sky, the posture, the iconography) would evoke the mood and meaning of the painting. Thus, the time of the day, the time of the year, context, emotion — the totality of aesthetic emotions being

---

16. Kaufmann, op. cit., pp. 276-77.
17. A tradition which goes back probably to *Rāgasāgara* in the ninth century CE. Ibid., p. 198.

evoked — would emerge. It also internalizes the obsession of Indian music with time, with specific points of time, with the necessity of maintaining propriety of time and the outrage one feels when "timeliness" is flouted.[18]

Rāgamālā tradition has many complexities. However, they will not be discussed here. For instance, a strong family metaphor runs through the tradition. Kaufmann points out that the classification of *rāga*s into male and female can be traced back to between seventh to eleventh century:

> With Nārada's *Saṅgita-Makaranda*, written some time between the seventh and eleventh centuries, begins the grouping of *rāga*s into male and female (*rāgiṇī*) types. Nārada does not yet use the term *rāgiṇī* but employs *strī* or *yoṣita* (woman).[19]

---

18. See Kaufmann for a historical exploration of the relation between music and time. Kaufmann also recounts an anecdote about Indian attitude to music and time even in the twentieth century that seems to profoundly have affected him: We shall abstain from repeating these often-told stories and from continuing this thought, except to relate one conversation I had with a very famous old Indian musician in Bombay in 1934. The old man said: "Do you know that you people in the West will soon experience a most terrible disaster? And do you know why?" When I shrugged my shoulders the grand old man thundered: "Because you people in the West abuse music and play it at wrong occasions and at wrong times! You play funeral marches and dirges when there is no funeral, you sing love songs and spring songs when there is neither love nor spring, you perform Nocturnes during the day and wedding music when there is no wedding! How long," he roared, "will the universe tolerate this abuse of music which, after all, is a sacred thing?" This, probably the most unusual reason ever offered as the cause for the outbreak of the second World War, illustrates better than all previous descriptions the ardent devotion and unshakeable beliefs old Indian musicians have in "that sacred thing," their music. p. 289.

19. Kaufmann, op. cit., p. 276.

In painting (where this concept was taken up after more than six centuries), there are six principal *rāgas*; each of these *rāgas* has five consorts (in some traditions more) called *rāgiṇīs* and even children (*rāgaputras*). The element of time as seasons gets reflected in the six principal *rāgas*, namely, *Bhairava*, *Dīpikā*, *Śrī*, *Mālkauṅsa*, *Megha* and *Hiṇḍolā*. These are meant to be sung during the six seasons of the year; summer, monsoon, autumn, early winter, winter and spring.[20] But, although diurnal time plays an important role in many *rāgas*, i.e. many *rāgas* are meant to be sung at specific times of the day or night — for instance, *Bhairava* (morning), *Haṁsadhvani* (evening), *Toḍī* (night) — this doesn't get systematically depicted in the Rāgamālā tradition.

As discussed earlier, art often depicts the passage of time or tries to capture the essence of a particular period or moment of time. The garland of *rāgas* in its structure represents cyclic time. In that sense, the structure internalizes the passage of time. As one moves from *rāga* to *rāga* and experiences the change of seasons, she experiences the cycle of a year as it vibrates through nature and the self.

On the other hand, each painting, in isolation, tries to capture the essence of a *rāga* or *rāgiṇī*. This essence can only be relished by the iconography, the gestures, the surrounding atmosphere and time which evoke the mood of the *rāga* or *rāgiṇī* and lead to aesthetic relish or *rasa*. Ideally, the "perfect" Rāgamālā painting would be able to evoke the cadence of the *rāga* in the ideal perceiver. In this sense it would have a share of the magical quality of Indian music of engendering time.

For instance, let us take *Toḍī rāgiṇī*. The iconography shows

---

20. See Harold Powers, "Illustrated Inventories of Indian Rāgamālā Painting", *Journal of the American Oriental Society*, vol. 100, no. 4, (October–December, 1980) pp. 473-93; "*Rāgamālā* Painting" www.wikepedia.org; also see Klaus, and Capwell.

a lady with a *vīṇā* amidst nature surrounded by animals and birds. The colour of the sky suggests that it is night — the time when *Toḍī* is sung (see image below).[21]

For one who is familiar with the tradition of Indian music and painting, the stillness of the white lilies at the bottom of the picture, the graceful and yet frozen posture of the lady, the posture of the birds and animals should evoke the languid beauty of this *rāga* of the late night.

21. The image is taken from Wikepedia essay "Rāgamālā Paintings," http://en.wikipedia.org/wiki/File:TodiRagini,Ragamala,Bundi, Rajasthan,1591.jpg.

The Rāgamālā tradition of paintings that has come down to us[22] is more than four hundred years old and many complete and incomplete series exist. While some of them are exquisite masterpieces, others are poor copies or renditions. One often finds contradictions such as improper depiction of time and outright flouting of the mood by presentation of emotions contrary to what is evoked by the *rāga*. However, in the best of the Rāgamālā paintings, one finds the assimilation of many complex art forms — namely music, dance, story telling — and the absorption of many conscious and unconscious dimensions of the very act of living within a tradition. It is because of this that Rāgamālā is a site for the exploration of time and its impact on human beings; for it is the confluence of different representations of time. Indian music echoes and vibrates with evocations of times of days and seasons. Indian paintings depict time variously through the very postures, gestures, the activities of various animals and plants and the sky itself. Thus, time pervades the Rāgamālā paintings, if not consciously, then unconsciously, like the act of breathing.

---

22. See Harold Powers, "Illustrated Inventories of Indian Rāgamālā Painting", *Journal of the American Oriental Society*, vol. 100, no. 4 (October–December 1980), pp. 473-93.

11

Time and Architecture

Dialogues — The Indian perspective

Joy Sen and *Joydeep Dutta*

Time and the Lost Ark — The Origin

In the Biblical tradition, the beginning of Time is Genesis and Noah's Ark. In India, it is the boat of Manu carrying the seed of the universe. Here the seed, the *Arka* (meaning the original sunrays) is anthropologically represented by the seven colours of creation or the seven patriarchal sages. Since then, time has always been an element of human association and also an icon of enigma, unfathomable perpetuity and impenetrability.

Today the concept of time lies at the heart of cosmology and physics. Whether it is Newtonian or Cartesian mechanical-fragmented time, or Einstein's famous relativistic time, its influence over all fields of knowledge and human activity has been centrally profound. So is the case of Architecture that expresses human concepts of time in a unique way. The range may vary from symbolism to realism — from the lighter to the darker side of time. This expression stretches from an abstract symbolism portraying the brightness of a lost glory or future time, to a hardcore reality representing the dire need of a particular time. Today, crisis and disaster management demands cost-effective solutions to be delivered at right time.

This is to face the ravages of nature, deterioration or obsolescence representing the darker side of time.

Contrasting both lighter and darker aspects of time, Indian aesthetics and functionalism ultimately take the user beyond both and allow him to see the origins of time. Indian architecture thus reserves its own way of perceiving time and expressing it conceptually — at an abstract level of the material manifest.[1] This article is an attempt to bring to light the Indian approach to understand "Time" or rather, the Indian architectural perspective of time.

Architecture and Time — The Basics

Architecture, down the ages, has been a carrier of time. Its movement is like a long diverse carriageway where individual wagons seem to contain parcels of elements, garnered by a particular patron, a "movement" or "style" of the given age. Space is contiguous with time. Differentiation in space determines the ticking of the clock and the normal cycles (circle) — day and night, seasons, ages, epochs and so on. Any undifferentiating movement is a break-off from the circle and a spiral seeking a dimensionless absolute or *bindu*. Such progressions could be instantaneous, momentary or changes stretching over long periods of time. This is the notion of space-time continuum. Architectural space may be considered to have four[2] successive hierarchical experiential stages in this continuum.

In the first stage, space is physical[3] and Cartesian. This is

1. The ideational space has been described vividly by Amos Rapoport in "The cultural origins of architecture", J.C. Snyder and A.J. Catanese, eds., *Introduction to Architecture* (New York: McGraw-Hill, 1979).
2. This is equivalent to the principle of Cosmic intelligence or *mahat*.
3. And this idea is closest to *prakṛti* (nature) of Sāṁkhya philosophy.

an area where material, realistic and conventional behavioural attributes of space usage are valid and time is cyclic. In the next stage, space is mental, habitual, ritual[4] and repetitive. Spaces are designed where functions recur for a higher purpose and the cycle attempts to break off from conventional movements and habits. Thirdly, space is cognitive and mythical. Here mental movements spiral off[5] to identify the present purpose with the past and future. Hence myths and histories are created. The backward and forward linkages are established. Finally in the fourth phase, space becomes all-pervasive and cosmological, where the journey realizes the

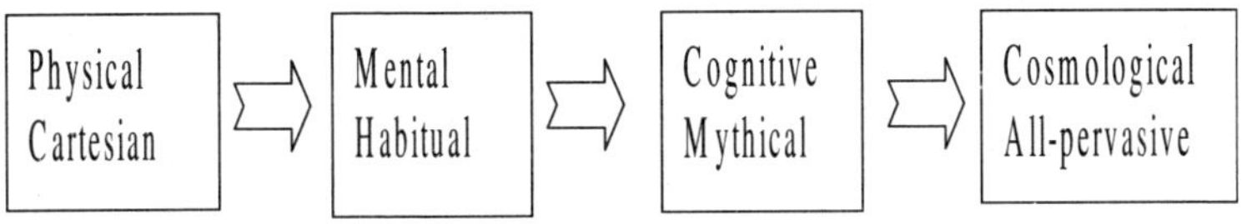

fig. 1: Four Stages of the Architectural Space-Time Continuum

grand purpose behind all purposes and functions. The centre of the universe — the *bindu* becomes synonymous with the centre of the user — the architect. This is the climax. Beyond this fourth and final stage, the spiral ladder collapses to the

4. This is equivalent to the simile in the *Gospel of Shri Ramakrishna*, where there are ten pots with water and the ten reflections of the one sun in the sky. The pots are destroyed one by one. After the ninth pot being destroyed, there is only one and last reflection left — last moving image of eternity. After the destruction of the last pot, there is no reflection left. But who will say that. At a material plane, the pot is the enclosure or the building. Ultimately, the pot represents the stages of human evolution going up to complete *nirvāṇa* or rapture with the Absolute (equivalent to Biblical Atonement).

5. Bertrand Russell, *A History of Western Philosophy*, (Routledge, 2nd edn., 2004), p. 158.

Bindu itself. In other words, the *bindu* expands to an ocean[6] of universal play and timeless unity.

Architecture that is Timeless — The Traditional Ethos

In Indian architecture, the original emphasis was on the non-domestic part considered to be sacred and timeless. Architecture for the common man or for domestication was relatively profane and subject to the ravages of time. In India, space, time, and matter are manifestations of the creator omnipotent. Material space and material things make visible the ideational behind.[7] For this the architectural movement is expected to have three ramifications.

First, it stresses a new theme of control — unprecedented in Western models of design. It stresses the fact that **one changes oneself in time rather than the environment.** The evolution of human function finally bordering the timeless is the ultimate aim. Thus, a building and its inherent architecture is a major modification of the material environment which requires rigorous adherence to a timeless cosmological plan and a ritual purity of the setting to which the function conforms.

Secondly, the cosmological layer of the material architectural plan emphasizes a centrality symbolizing this changeless and therefore an origin of the universe, that is perhaps timeless.

---

6. It is the Expression of *tamo guṇa* as compared to *rajo* and *sattva guṇa*, which represents non-inert (dynamic) and refined or sublime non-inert (contemplative and intuitive) nature of reality or *prakṛti*.

7. Refer article, "The Paithrukam of Indo-European Language" in Seminar-workshop (October 2002) magazine, *Paithrukam* (Ancestral) organized by MES School of Architecture, Kuttipuram, p. 110.

Thirdly, symbols are incorporated every time to manifest the ideational behind the real. Through repetition and rhythm of these symbols, the architecture touches the *puruṣa* — the timeless. Space is transformed by these elements. Elements of an outer gross form are introduced the last time as the user steps into the inner form to realize subtle design elements for the first time. In gradations and sequences, the journey culminates from the outer to the inner and finally the innermost — the *sanctum sanctorum* where the timeless is made visible. Architecture in this sense transforms all material objects or *vāstu* to a rhythmic organic whole called the *vāstu*.

In the earliest phases of ancient Greek architecture, such considerations were also visible. In Plato's *Timaeus* we get a final account on the origin of Time:

> . . . The creator-father[8] created images of eternal gods, he rejoiced, and in this joy determined to make copy still more like the original; and this was eternal, he sought to make the universe eternal, so far as might be. Now the nature of the ideal being was everlasting (eternal as a flux and not in essence),[9] but to bestow this attribute in its fullness upon a creature was impossible. Wherever he resolved to have a moving image of eternity, and when set in order the heaven, he made this image eternal but moving (so that as an image it can be eternal in its immanence or movement), according to number, while eternity itself rests in unity (the

8. Refer article, "Scientist and Electrician Nichola Tesla" in Ramkrishna Mission Institute of Culture June 2002 Bulletin for detail explanation of the cycles of time and going in and going out within the Cosmic "word" itself. Tesla met Swami Vivekananda in 1893 during the City beautiful movement and Columbian exposition in Chicago. Tesla is also the father of alternating current.

9. From "Cosmology", *Complete Works of Swami Vivekananda*, vol. 2, (pp. 435-36) explaining concurrences, repetitions and rhythms.

> transcendental opposed to or mirror to the immanent); and this image[10] we call Time.[11]

Of the eternal aspect, there is neither "it was" or "will be" and therefore we cannot say that. But of the "moving Image of eternity," it is correct to say that "it was" and "it will be" and this is "Time in its backward and forward linkages." The backward linkage, is going back to history. The forward linkage is a journey unto future. In this moving image there is therefore the knowledge of numbers and the unity of opposites of the two linkages, i.e. of that, which was and which will be. This comes closest to the concept of *puruṣa* or *prakṛti*. *Puruṣa* is in the eternal sense standing unchanging and therefore timeless. *Prakṛti* is in the movement, the changes in space and time, in the eternal rings of concentric patterns or the *maṇḍala*.

The concept of time is fundamental to both Indian philosophy and Western sciences. At the root of Indian architecture stand the eternal timeless *puruṣa* and the concentric manifestations or ripples, which is *prakṛti* or functions in space or nature itself. Manifestations in space are gross and inert in expression as they are built out of the most tangible materials of creation like mud, brick, glass or concrete. In the Indian viewpoint, such manifestations are called *tāmasika* or expressions of gross inertia. The concept of Time in this grossest sense is a function of this inert existence or *Prakṛti* itself in the *tāmasika* form[12] (an expression of *tamo guṇa* as compared to *rajo* and *sattva guṇa*, which represents non-inert

10. Cf. Augustine's reflections where he distinguishes the "longitudinal" aspects *extensio* and *distensio* from the vertical aspects *attentio* and *intentio*, all of them dimensions of the temporal reality and directly connected with *actio*.

11. The ideas have been derived from part 8: space as the Extension of Existence (pages 24-25) in R. Pannikar's "There is no outer without inner space", *Concept of Space* (IGNCA).

12. This is equivalent to absolute Śruti and relative planes of Smṛti.

(dynamic) and refined or sublime non-inert (contemplative and intuitive) nature of reality or *prakr̥ti*).

The word *tama* means the gross inertia of the ever-changing and ever moving material universe in eternal flux. And Time exactly denotes the sum-total gross inertia of a universe of multiplicity or numbers. Here the essence of *tama* also represents that of Time.[13] *Tama* thus represents the embodied soul imbedded in the bondage of matter but ready for a fresh release into another half-cycle of creation going back to its roots. Probably, imbedded in the word *tama* is the concept of cosmic time (*kalpa*).[14]

The blowing in and the blowing out of the Universe (signifying the ascent of spirit from matter and its descent into matter again) are described on the basis of *prāṇa* (life or conscious energy of the user) and *ākāśa* (space itself). On this we may quote:

> . . . When the *kalpa* begins, after an immense interval, the *anidavatam* (unvibrating stage) commences to vibrate and blow after blow is given by *prāṇa* to *ākāśa*. . . . The *ākāśa*, acted upon by repeated blows of *prāṇa*, produces *vāyu* or vibrations. This *vāyu* vibrates, and the vibrations growing more and more rapid result in friction giving rise to heat or *tejas*. Then the heat ends in liquefaction, *āpaḥ* or *jalaḥ*. Then that liquid becomes solid (gross inertia or the stage of *tamas*) and it goes back in exactly the same way.[15]

Thus, architecture of the Cosmos involving the five basic

13. Cf. A.L. Basham, "Chapter VIII: The Spirit in Indian art" *The Wonder that was India* (New Delhi: Rupa, 1981).

14. The idea has been taken from an analysis done by John M. Fritz and George Michell in their article entitled: "Space and Meaning in Vijaynagara" in *Concept of Space: Ancient and Modern*, ed. Kapila Vatsayan (New Delhi: IGNCA, 1991).

15. This is equivalent to the *pañca-bhūtas* or the five gross elements of physical reality (like *kṣiti, apa* . . .)

ingredients are also manifest in the architecture of the small or individual buildings, which are also created to sustain for a period of time and then they are withering off in similar pattern or cycles. The ancients had observed this concurrence and from their wisdom sprang the knowledge of *puruṣa* and *maṇḍala* imbedded both in the vast (macro-cosmos) and the small (microcosm). In this sense, Indian architecture had always represented more of a human journey rather than a simple function attempting to touch something beyond space and time — the Timeless or *puruṣa* itself.

Extended in Space (Architecture) — Distended in Time

Augustine had described time as a certain distension[16] of our existence (in a non-cartesian way) and recovers the word-extension calling it space. We are and we exist distended in time and extended in space. Existence is both (temporal) distension and (spatial) extension. There is a specific sense of human time that we call temporality. Similarly, the specific human space is called spatiality. In Western tradition, from Augustine to Heidegger, the temporal character has been profusely reflected.

The Indo-Vedic traditions are equally full of wisdom about the nature of time. Human fullness implies the synthesis of the three times (present continuous and the backward and forward linkages) and/or the overcoming of time. Death, birth, *karma* and salvation are all basic notions with respect to time. Architectural spatial functions like a cemetery, a hospital, an institution and an *āśrama* are correspondences to such notions. Human existence is a temporal pilgrimage — it is distended temporally. Time pervades everything and is the coefficient of our Cartesian fragmentation — the symbol of

16. This is equivalent to the *pañca-tanmātras* or the five subtle elements of subtle reality (like *rūpa, rasa* . . .).

our contingency.[17] The absolute is concerned to be eternal, timeless and also at times, timeful. Architecture dedicated to the absolute is likewise timeless and "timeful." Architecture dedicated to the relative is a pilgrimage to the absolute — a moving image of "eternity" proceeding from the relative.

Architecture-Time reflections are mnemonic — they aid our memory and germinate a sense of continuity, a rhythm of life itself in perception. Symbols, icons and space-forms recur and repeat themselves — sometimes in harmonious transition, sometimes in rampant ignorant copying of architectural elements. The built forms of Indian architecture serve as a repetitive tribute to the "ascent of humanity." The memories of the past transform and evolve as the future rhythms. They evolve and re-evolve as cycles — ranging from a year (solar equinoctial or time of microcosm) to a *saṁvatsara* (seasonal cycles) or a *kalpa* (birth and dissolution of universe or the macrocosm), which is Platonic *aeon*. The expressions are different but the essence the same.[18] The music in the celestial firmament is echoed in the frozen harmonies and rhythms of the spaces designed on the mother earth. Each expression and functionalism in space is ultimately a part of that eternal movement — that infinite musical wave. It may be therefore said:

Perpetuity is Time — from eternity to eternity.
Infinity is Space — the wave of Time itself.
One is inseparable from the other.
Where one exists not, the other too.
The stillness is "Thou Art That"
Around which they remain ever
As the dance of the two is Architecture.

17. This is equivalent to psychic *prāṇa* itself represented by neural electricity (*vidyuta*) like currents.

18. This is equivalent to the vast reservoir of Universal or cosmic *prāṇa* called the *mahat*.

12

Portrayal of Time in Indian Popular Music

Amrita Basu

THIS article aims to study the portrayal of Time in the field of Indian popular music. Time, as a category, has attracted attention in most cultures — ancient and modern, classical and popular; and it has always resisted any attempt at definition. Indian culture with its rich tradition is one where Time pervades almost all its dimensions. Therefore, an examination of how Time has been treated or portrayed in Indian popular culture would be interesting. The field of popular culture is taken for study since it is felt that the long and continuing Indian tradition has had pervasive influence on all the fields of contemporary popular culture.

Popular culture is a vast field for it comprises popular music, dance, screen mediums, etc. Among these fields, popular music is a category which finds expression in ancient arts like dance, drama,[1] and also in modern arts like Indian cinema, and in other screen mediums like soaps and music videos. Thus, it is a field which has a significant presence in today's cultural scenario. Music extends itself in time, has rhythm which is

1. Music and its relation to dance and drama can be traced back to Bharata's *Nāṭyaśāstra*.

cyclic and is a complex of tone, tempo and lyric where the text can also refer to time. Hence, an exploration of the treatment of time in Indian popular music, it is expected, would provide us with some interesting insights.[2]

Indian Music Tradition and Popular Music

Music forms an integral part of Indian tradition. Some of the most ancient texts — including parts of the Vedas — were meant to be sung or recited in certain ways and incorporated the use of notes, melody and rhythm. The fundamentals of Indian classical music can be traced to the *Sāmaveda* with the use of the fundamental notes. Later on the *Nāṭyaśāstra* took up the discussion of music in a significant way and music was thus acknowledged as an element that was deeply linked to our performative tradition of plays, enactments and dance.

If we look at our folk tradition and their observance of various rituals related to plantation, harvest, etc. music played and still plays a very important role. Most traditional forms of folk performance use songs and music. Many festivals as well as personal celebrations in our tradition have songs, music and dance as their integral part — the most noticeable in today's context, especially popular culture, being *bhāṅgṛā* and *garbā*.

---

2. For many of the ideas here I am indebted to the following sources: (1) Philip Alperson, " 'Musical Time' and Music as an 'Art of Time' ", *The Journal of Aesthetics and Art Criticism*, Summer 1980, pp. 441; (2) Edward T. Hall, *The Dance of Life* (New York: Anchor Press/ Doubleday, 1983); (3) Monelle, Raymond "Deconstruction and Allegory", *Linguistics and Semintics in Music* (Chur: Harwood Academic Publishers, (1992). pp. 304-23; (4) Mukund Lath, "The 'Modern', the 'Traditional', and 'Criticism in the Indian Musical Tradition' ", *Sangeet Natak*, 89-90, December 1988; (5) Sushil Kumar Saxena, "Hindustani Rhythm and An Aesthetical Issue", *Sangeet Natak*, New Delhi, nos. 129–130, 1998, pp. 34–37.

However, when one speaks about popular culture today, the most popular category in music is neither classical music nor folk songs; it is "the film song." Songs have become synonymous with Indian film culture. Each film has at least six songs to its credit, not to mention the musicals which have thirteen or fourteen songs. And it is not just restricted to the mainstream Hindi film. Even regional films have a large number of them. Songs often act as filler programmes in many television channels in addition to channels exclusively devoted to music. Popular songs are used while reversing cars, receiving calls on mobiles, and it has indeed a huge audience.

India also has a very rich tradition of music videos/albums which are aired simultaneously with film songs. Although the idea was borrowed from the West, especially with the advent of MTV in India during the 1990s, later we saw a major upsurge of local talents, and today most music channels air Indian music videos and film songs. These also form a considerable part of popular music and share almost the same popularity as film songs. The film song and the music album dominate today's popular Indian music. Though serials and advertisements also contain songs, in their case, these songs are used to sell particular products, or are played only when the serial starts and the titles are shown. Therefore, only the film song clips and the music album clips will be considered under the category of popular music in this article.

The next sections would attempt to explore how Indian popular music integrates time; and if our culture and music tradition influences this integration.

Time and Indian Popular Music

Apparently, popular music, especially film music, often uses many cinematographic techniques linked to portrayal of time — namely, dream sequences, flashbacks, etc. But these cinematographic narrative techniques reflecting portrayal of time do not form the basis of our study because, one, they are found almost globally in the medium of cinema and soaps; two, techniques often have to do with technology, and therefore at one point of time, most media use the latest technology; three, studying them would involve a detailed study of the narrative of films, which is not the aim of the article. Moreover, the music album may not be related to a master narrative unlike the film song. Therefore techniques like flashback, etc. are left out in this chapter — it chiefly focuses on how time in our tradition gets reflected in these instances of Indian popular music.

The first and foremost issue here is finding out whether there are popular songs which have time as their very theme. In the cultural history of modern India there is a rich tradition of films which have been named after Time or refer to Time in their titles — *Waqt* (1965),[3] *Samaya,*[4] etc. where the songs (e.g. *ek pal ki* from *Samaya* which is about time running out) talk about the power of time. Songs on reincarnation themes from films like *Nagīnā* (1986) (song: *bhūlī bisarī prema kahānī*), *Ab ke Baras* (2002) (song: *āyā māhī āyā*), *Banjāran* (1991) (song: *mai banjāran rastā dekhe*) and songs from music albums like *Noorie* (1979) (song: *ā jā re*) often portray the present as a product of actions of past lives. In these cases, popular songs become texts which portray the doctrine of *karma,* a very ancient and predominant belief in India. These songs, incidentally, often contain some supernatural and unexplainable characters like spirits who belong to both worlds past and present. Characters in myths and legends move from one time-world to another effortlessly and come back from where they started. Thus,

3. Hindi movie released in 1965.

4. A relatively recent Hindi movie released in 2003.

every action becomes relational in the world of time (which includes the past, present and future) in these popular songs.

Time Through Visual and Lyrics

Continuing with our exploration into the stylistic features of music videos, we shall now proceed to examine the visual depiction of time in popular songs. Time is most commonly depicted through geographical locations shown in popular songs. For example, many songs take place in ruins and seashores. Songs like *tere mere bīca meiṅ* from *Ek Dūje Ke Liye* (1981) take place in ruins and seashores; they foreshadow the future of the lovers and at the same time portray the everlasting quality of their love amidst the ebb and flow of life. Here, time is indicated through a combination of visual and lyrical symbols.

Some popular songs also consciously use the style of presenting a song by juxtaposing black and white and colour modes in order to show the presence or absence of joy in a person's life. Anuradha Paudwal's music video *Beete Din Beete Pal* (1999) is a case in point where the present life of the woman character is depicted in black and white and her past life (when her fiancé was alive) is presented in colour. Thus, a very common strategy of depicting past and present is consciously reversed.

This interplay of the past and present is also observed in portraying the effect of time on the human body and attitudes in songs like *tere liye hum hai jiye* from film *Veer Zārā* (2004). In this song, two elderly people meet at the courtroom, but the focus shifts between their bodies in old age and in youth. To each, the other still appears as if he or she is very young. Even their attitudes are shown not to have changed with time; the man has preserved an anklet of the woman who in turn has been wearing only one anklet all her life. So, the change of focus from black and white to colour, or from old age to youth reflects the subjective interpretation of time. Though this element is not intrinsically linked to Indian culture, it gives us an awareness of the Indian mind's constant reflection on time, even in popular songs.

Depiction of monsoon, spring and late evenings abound in popular songs; other periods of the day and seasons also find mention in popular numbers. For example, *kahīn dūra jaba din ḍhala jāye* is sung in *Anand* (1970) by a patient terminally ill. Here, the song makes use of the late afternoon and early evening time to show that time is running out. He also looks at an autumnal leaf in a very intense manner, being terminally ill; he is at the autumn of his life. Thus, the passage of time is depicted here.

This kind of subjective interpretation of time is also achieved in another unique way by Shankar Mahadevan's music video *Breathless* (1999). The song continues without the singer stopping or gasping for a single breath. There is continuity of the song throughout and only at the end, when the song ends does the singer stop and give out a sound resembling "phew." Instead of taking in breath, he lets it out. There is an ironic play on the title *Breathless* and time comes into the audience's mind in a significant way since it waits for the singer to take a breath in vain. It is the listener who is finally breathless.

Time and Seasons in Rāgas and Popular Songs

Another prominent feature of Indian popular songs is that they often depict the season or the time of the day in the visuals and sometimes directly in the lyrics. Now, seasons and times of the day formed an important part of the music tradition in India, namely in the tradition of the *rāga*s. A short note on the *rāga* tradition and its basis in time seems appropriate before venturing into the depiction of time, days and seasons in popular songs.

Rāga (structure of melody) and *tāla* (structure of rhythm) are two major elements that characterize Indian Classical music. The melody deals with the rise and fall of notes and the *tāla* is concerned with rhythm — patterns of beats to time that often accompany the *rāga*s. Time is a commanding presence in the *rāga*s also because some *rāga*s are meant to be sung at particular times of the day and some are meant for particular seasons only. It is assumed that each *rāga* manages to evoke the mood of a particular time of the day or year. Hence, it is most apt to perform it at that point of time. On the other hand, this also can imply that by performing a *rāga* at any point of time, the mood of a particular time of the day or year can also be evoked.

There are *rāga*s for all *prahara* (different times of the cycle of a day), i.e. from early morning till late in the night. To name a few: *rāga Lalita* is related to the time before dawn, *rāga Multānī* is best sung late in the afternoon, i.e. before sunset. *Bihāga, Bāgeśvarī, Mālkauṁsa* are *rāga*s suited for night and late night. In other words, time/seasons and their impact on human emotions are also explored in this way. For example, *Haṁsadhvani*, which is an early evening *rāga* is quick and joyous in nature, while *Darabārī*, a late night *rāga* is slow and erotic in its evocation.

Similarly, to quote a few examples of *rāga*s related to seasons, *Bahāra* (which consists of sub-categories like *Bahāra, Adhāna Bahāra, Sura Bahāra* and *Basanta Bahāra*) group of *rāga*s is sung for the spring season, just as the *Malhāra* (which consists of subcategories *Malhāra (Śuddha), Megha Malhāra, Miyān kī Malhāra, Mīrā kī Malhāra, Sura Malhāra*) group of *rāga*s is meant for the rains. Thus, there are fixed *rāga*s for particular times of the day as well as particular times of the year.

While tradition considers that *rāga*s sung out of season can imbalance nature and lead to dire consequences — as illustrated by the famous legend of Tansen singing the *Dīpaka rāga* and setting everything on fire including himself, with only his student's rendition of the *Megha Malhāra* bringing relief — in Indian popular music this is not strictly adhered to.

Popular music in India has numerous examples which are related to time in two distinctive ways — they are based on the *rāga*s of specific times or season; or else the lyric evokes a particular time of the day or year. Often we find that visual, lyric and *rāga* are integrated in popular songs to evoke a specific time of day or year.

Many popular songs in India refer to time in their lyrics or depict seasons like spring and monsoon and times of the day like evening and late evening. Songs like *suno sajanā āye din bahāra ke* from *Āye Din Bahāra Ke* (1966) or songs like *śāma gayī rāta āyī ke bālam ā jā* from the film, *Shree 420* (1955) are cases in point. So, here, popular culture has drawn on elements from the *rāga* tradition which also often uses late evening *rāga*s to portray love and romance.

Songs about monsoon like *Abke Sāvana Aise Barase* (1999), a music video by Shubha Mudgal explores this romantic angle and its relation to monsoon. The music is set to a monsoon *rāga*. The video initially depicts daytime and how each character is leading a very boring existence. Dark clouds come into the picture and the song starts with the first drops of rain. And then it picks up pace and talks about lovers meeting, visually depicts a young couple coming out and dancing, etc. So the song celebrates the coming of the first rain after a hot summer as a time for celebration, happiness, meeting one's lover, etc. It would not be wrong to link this to the tradition of Rāgamālā paintings (which again tried to visually depict the mood of certain *rāgas*) where rain is often linked to the union of lovers.

Similarly, morning finds expression as a time which is full of promise and hope in popular music. This is also borrowed from the *rāga* tradition. The song *woh subaha kabhi to āyegī* (1956) is about hope in the midst of depression and *subaha* is morning, which is full of hope. The song *jāgo mohana pyāre* (1956) has for its setting morning when a lady waters the plants and also quenches the hero's thirst for ideal goodness after a night full of experiences with tricksters and conmen (*Jāgte Raho*, 1956). It is in *Bhairava* which is an early morning *rāga*. So, the human body and phase of the day seen in the body itself are drawn from the ancient Indian tradition of the body-nature relation, the microcosm-macrocosm relation as far as the portrayal of time is concerned.

Religious and Film Songs, Festivals and the Decontextualization of Time

Popular songs having religious fervour like *bhajanas*, devotional music, etc. are also set to particular times of the day. For morning *pūjā* a particular kind of verse and ritual is apt, for evening a different one is required. For example, we have *sandhyā bhajanas*, and *prātaḥ bhajanas*.

However, there is one point which is of great importance in these songs. While the visual depiction is that of a particular period of day or year and the songs are often set to specific *rāgas*, the public listens to (and watches) all these music at various times of the day or night. This brings in the concept of decontextualization of time, where anything fixed for being performed at a particular time is repeated or performed out of the context. So, what about the representation of time here? Since we just mentioned the case of popular religious songs in

India belonging to categories like *sandhyā bhajanas* and *prātaḥ bhajanas*, an exploration of popular songs during festivals in India, and their process of decontextualization would be also interesting.

There are many festivals in India and music and dance form a significant part of the celebrations. For example, every year, as homage to the Goddess, *Dussehra* and *Dūrgā Pūjā* are celebrated. *Dīwalī*, *Holī* and *Ṛākhī* are also celebrated with pomp and grandeur though not with the same kind of grandeur we associate with *Dūrgā Pūjā* or *Navrātrī*. All these festivals involve songs and dances. A point to be noted here is that some festivals are spread over days — *Navrātrī* as the name suggests is celebrated over nine nights; *Dūrgā Pūjā*, *Dussehra* continues for ten days. Some on the other hand are observed on particular auspicious days. It would provide revealing insights if we see how this theme is developed in popular songs.

Films like *Āp Mujhe Acche Lagne Lage* (2002), use various days of the *Navrātrī* festival to show the development of love between the onscreen couple. The first day of *Navrātrī* uses a song "Hindaroo" which involves *garbā* beats and community participation. This is aptly used because the participatory aspect of the song brings the lead pair together. Towards the end of the nine days, the title song *āp mujhe acche lagne lage* comes up where the lead pair confess their love for each other. So, the development of affection during a particular auspicious time period is portrayed through songs in the movie. This method is also used in *Devdas* (2002) where the song *ḍolā re ḍolā re* is used to portray the love of the two leading ladies for the hero and the climax.

As we have already marked, some festivals are spread over days, while some festivals are celebrated on particular auspicious days. Now, those which are spread over a few days like *Durgā Pūjā*, *Navrātrī*, etc. are community-oriented celebrations. Festivals like *Rākhī* and *Holī* on the other hand, involve interaction with the community but are more personal-relationship oriented. The relation between brother and sister, close friends, lovers, etc. find a high incidence in events related to these festivals. Often these also find expression in songs and dances used to express these festivals, and the portrayal of time there becomes an important area of study in popular culture.

For example, in many popular songs about *Holī* (*Sholay* (1975) — *holī ke din; Kaṭī Pataṅg* (1970) — *āj khele holī*), while people are seen celebrating, a widow stands alone somewhere at a distance without having a single splash of colour. Similarly, in many popular songs, at a point of crisis the hero or the supporting hero splashes colour on the widowed heroine which is an indication of the change that is going to come in the heroine's life. Thus, at the beginning of the song, the time for celebration for people in these songs is also a time that brings out the difference in the condition of the widowed character concerned. It denies her the celebration. But being a very auspicious day, it brings in auspicious moments in the widowed character's life; new love comes to her life. This is often explored in popular songs symbolically.

Rakṣā bandhana and its celebration also find expression in popular songs. Songs like, *rākhī ke din bhaiyā tum vādā nibhānā* (*Reśama kī Ḍorī*, 1974) portrays the time of promises which the brother makes to his sister. Later in the film concerned, the brother is shown going against all odds to protect his sister, thereafter keeping his promise. So the time of this auspicious day for *Rākhī* acts as a pre-indicator, thus bringing in the ancient Indian concept of premonitions, forebodings, etc. where attempts are made to look into the time that is about to come.

Festivals that are to be celebrated in particular time of

the year have already been discussed. But in addition to festivals, there are numerous festivities also in a person's life. Music and dance are associated with marriage, birth, sometimes even death. In the Indian religious context, sacred time (*muhūrtta*) has been discussed as a very important concept. There are auspicious moments and inauspicious moments, especially in the performance of rituals in the context of birth, death, thread ceremony, marriage, house building — virtually every part of life.

Similarly, there are appropriate time periods for certain kinds of activities. For example, in the case of marriage, one particular day is reserved for *haldī* ceremony (where the bride is covered in turmeric paste); one for *mehandī*, one for marriage, this often extends to pre-marriage and post-marriage celebrations. For example, welcoming the new bride in the family is a post-marriage celebration. All these are also depicted in popular songs. The *Varmala Music Video Series* by T-Series for example, show all aspects of marriage through the medium of songs. There are also many popular songs which celebrate the time of engagement in similar ways. Some cases in point are: *mai sasurāla nahī jāūṅgī* (*Chandni*, 1989), *mai tere khayāloṅ me* (*Tridev*, 1989), etc.

In fact, nowadays, more and more songs are seen celebrating engagements rather than marriages. This was not celebrated in the Indian cultural scenario initially with so much elan. These have now become areas where music and dance and celebrations have come in more than they were traditionally present. And they are presented in the same style as marriages are presented. It might be said that times of marriage, ceremonies, etc. have been decontextualized and brought to suit the times of engagements in these music visuals. This, in a way, illustrates the flexibility of time in the Indian context. Engagement is at least related to marriage, but what about songs used to celebrate childbirth, harvest, etc. which have totally lost their context in recent times?

There are many music videos (especially *bhāṅgṛā* videos) which have no naturalistic hint of Time. For example, the video *Tunak tunak Tun* (Daler Mehndi, 1996), *Ḍhol Wajdā* (Sarabjit), *Cā Cā Cā* (Asha Bhosle, 2005), etc. never hint at which season or Time of the day it is. It is a total created environment. Only the performer is a constant feature. Seen from one angle, in these popular songs, the performer is central, which might also be used to suggest that the performer has left or come out of the restrictions imposed by Time.

Conclusion

The portrayal of Time in the field of Indian popular music is a reflection of the all embracing nature of Indian culture. In the cultural history of India there is a rich tradition of films which have been named after Time or refer to Time in their titles. There have also been some period films which are basically about a culture or an ethos passing away, the songs used in bringing out this passing away of periods. Songs, especially those on reincarnation themes, convey the cyclic narrative tradition in storytelling which we find in numerous Indian myths and legends.

The portrayal of time is achieved in Indian popular music in many ways. It is achieved through the depiction of the body as a significant site where changes in attitudes, emotions, and phases in life portray changes in time. So, the human body and its relation to phases of the day or of life which is often portrayed in popular songs can be said to reflect the ancient tradition of the body-nature relation, the microcosm-macrocosm relation in nature.

Not just the human body but also geographical locations

like ruins, seashores, etc. are used to portray destruction and rejuvenation, which form a part of the Indian concept of ebb and flow in life and after life. Time also becomes a subjective category in popular songs that consciously use the black and white mode of presentation, where the individual's state of mind and emotions influence his interpretation of time.

As various *rāgas* have been traditionally associated with various seasons and times of the day like morning and evening, many songs talk about the morning time (often one of hope of moving ahead in life and love) and evening time (waiting for the beloved, separation), etc. Songs on the rainy season, and on Spring are significantly high in number. Songs related to autumn on the other hand get related to various autumnal festivals and also personal festivities which bring in the concept of auspicious time or *śubha muhūrtta,* very specific to the Indian cultural scenario. This concept of auspicious time also forms the basis for the popular songs which celebrate marriages. However, they are often decontextualized to include engagements and even personal celebrations where there is no hint as to which season or time of the day it is.

To sum up, it can be said that the portrayal of time in the field of Indian popular music not only presents the elusiveness of time but also the all-encompassing nature of Indian culture.

The Contributors

Basu, (Dr.) Amrita is Lecturer, Department of MBA, Haldia Institute of Technology, Haldia, West Bengal. She is also a Ph.D scholar at the Department of Humanities & Social Sciences, IIT, Kharagpur. Her areas of research include Popular Culture and Women Studies [*e-mail*: 2009amrita@gmail.com].

Dutta, (Dr.) Joydeep is an architect working with TAJ Group of Hotels, Mumbai. Formerly he was a faculty at Department of Architecture and Regional Planning, IIT, Kharagpur. His areas of interest include Urban Planning and Architectural Design [*e-mail*: j_dutta@hotmail.com].

Komalesha, (Dr.) H.S. is Assistant Professor, Department of Humanities & Social Sciences, Indian Institute of Technology, Kharagpur. His areas of research include Colonial and Post-colonial studies. He is also a translator [*e-mail*: komalesha@yahoo.com].

Manjaly, (Dr.) Jaison A. is Assistant Professor, Department of Humanities & Social Sciences, Indian Institute of Technology, Gandhinagar. His areas of interest include Cognitive Philosophy and Sciences [*e-mail*: jmanjaly@gmail.com].

Mohanty, Late (Dr.) Niranjan was Professor, Department of English, Visva Bharati, Santiniketan. He was also eminent poet and translator.

Mohapatra, (Dr.) Bimalaprasad is a painter and sculptor. He is Reader, School of Commerce and Management Studies, Ravenshaw University, Cuttack.

Mukhopadhyay, (Dr.) P.K. is an eminent philosopher. Formerly Professor and Professor Emeritus at the Department of Philosophy, Jadavpur University, he currently lives at Varanasi. His areas of expertise include Indian Philosophy and Philosophy of Science.

Panda, (Dr.) G.P. is a Scholar of Sanskrit and Grammar. He has done considerable work on Time in Indian Grammatical Tradition. He lives at Delhi.

Paranjape, (Dr.) Binda is Reader, Department of History, Banaras Hindu University Varanasi. Her areas of interest include Culture Studies and Epigraphy [*e-mail*: binda_bhu@rediffmail.com].

Patnaik, (Dr.) Priyadarshi is Associate Professor, Department of Humanities & Social Sciences, Indian Institute of Technology, Kharagpur. His areas of interest include Indian Aesthetics, Visual Aesthetics and Nonverbal Communication [*e-mail*: priyadarshi1@yahoo.com].

Patnaik, (Dr.) Tandra retired as Professor, Department of Philosophy, Utkal University. Her areas of work include Philosophy of Language, Orissan Philosophical Tradition and *Bhakti* Philosophy of Orissa. She lives at Puri [*e-mail*: patnaik.tandra@yahoo.com].

Saha, (Dr.) Sukha Ranjan is an eminent philosopher. Formerly Professor and Professor Emeritus at the Department of Philosophy, Jadavpur University, he currently lives at Kolkata. His areas of expertise include Indian Philosophy.

Saxena, (Prof.) Sushil Kumar is an eminent aesthetician who has contributed significantly to the fields of Poetics, Aesthetics of Music and Dance. He was formerly professor at the Department of Philosophy, Delhi University. He lives at Delhi.

Sen, (Dr.) Joy is Associate Professor, Department of Architecture and Regional Planning, Indian Institute of Technology, Kharagpur. His areas of interest include Architectural Heritage Studies, City Planning and Indology [*e-mail*: joysen@arp.iitkgp.ernet.in].

Index